HOME ECONOMICS REVISION NOTES FOR LEAVING CERTIFICATE

MARY ANNE HALTON

GILL & MACMILLAN

Gill & Macmillan Ltd
Hume Avenue
Park West
Dublin 12
with associated companies throughout the world
www.gillmacmillan.ie

© Mary Anne Halton 1999, 2000

0 7171 3035 5

Print origination in Ireland by Carole Lynch, Dublin

The paper used in this book is made from the wood pulp of managed forests. For every tree felled, at least one tree is planted, thereby renewing natural resources.

All rights reserved.
No part of this publication may be reproduced, copied or transmitted in any form or by any means without written permission of the publishers or else under the terms of any licence permitting limited copying issued by the Irish Copyright Licensing Agency, The Writers' Centre, Parnell Square, Dublin 1.

CONTENTS

Introduction: Preparing for the Examination   vii

PART I: SCIENTIFIC

1. The Nutrients   1
2. Micro-nutrients   13
3. Additives, Enzymes, Colour and Flavour of Food   26
4. Planning Balanced Diets   31
5. Nutrition of Food   41
6. Microbiology   73
7. Food Preservation   85
8. Human Physiology   93

PART II: SOCIAL

II A: A PLACE TO LIVE

9. Housing   131
10. Services   139
11. Interior Design and Room Planning   157
12. Household Appliances   170
13. Consumer Education   185
14. Money Management   190

II B: SOCIOLOGY

15. Family, Relationships and Marriage   197
16. Problems in Families, Communities and Society   209
17. Child Development and Education   219
18. Community and Community Issues   223
19. Our World Today   228
20. Previous Questions to Practice   234

Past Examination Papers   238

INTRODUCTION
PREPARING FOR THE EXAMINATION

REVISION

When revising for the examination be positive. Take care of your health as part of exam preparation. Ensure that you have a balanced diet, sufficient rest, daily exercise and adequate sleep.

Allocate time for review and revision at the end of each week, month and term. The final revision should begin about 8 to 10 weeks before the examination. Develop speed and accuracy by practising writing questions and sketching diagrams. Adequate preparation will develop the confidence needed for the examination.

REVISION INVOLVES:

- Following the advice given by your teacher
- Analysing the format of previous papers
- Learning to understand the language used
- Developing good answering techniques
- Learning key points, concepts, avoiding waffle
- Practising and labelling diagrams
- Learning recipes that can be used in a number of answers
- Learning and using the relevant terminology
- Practising answering questions (*Writing* and *Timing*)
- Learning to be in control when answering questions

Learning from the 'Mock Exams' is important as part of the preparation. Identify your strengths and weaknesses at that time.

Keep up to date with the changes in society, cost of food, equipment, changes in the budget relating to consumer matters e.g. housing, taxes, welfare benefits. Some changes that occur may not be in your text book.

FORMAT OF THE HOME ECONOMICS EXAMINATION PAPER

There are two Sections:
Section I   Scientific
Section II   Social

NUMBER OF QUESTIONS ON PAPER

There are nine questions on the paper:
Section I   4 questions
Section II   5 questions
All students must answer a total of 5 questions.

STUDENTS TAKING HIGHER LEVEL PAPERS MUST SELECT:

- Two questions from Section I
- Two questions from Section II
- Other question from either Section

STUDENTS TAKING ORDINARY LEVEL PAPERS MUST SELECT:

- One question from Section I
- One question from Section II
- Other three questions from either Section

TIME ALLOWED

Higher and Ordinary Levels, 2 hours 45 minutes

MARKS ALLOWED

Total allocated is 400 marks. All questions carry 80 marks. The marks are then divided among each sub-section of each question. Answer all sections of each question.

KEY WORDS AND PHRASES FROM PREVIOUS QUESTIONS

When answering previous questions note key words and phrases that ask you:
- For specific information e.g. elemental composition, chemical structure
- To analyse e.g. assess, compare, discuss, differentiate, criteria
- To state facts e.g. outline, classify, specify, name, enumerate, function
- For details e.g. describe, explain, give an account, informative note
- For your opinion (make sure to back it up with accurate facts)

INTRODUCTION

PRESENTING WRITTEN ANSWERS

Help the examiner by presenting your work correctly numbered, neatly and clearly written, using well labelled diagrams where appropriate. Watch your handwriting, keep it neat.

- Number each question
- Number each subsection of each question
- Leave spaces between each subsection and each question
- Answer questions in point form, providing extra information with each point where required or appropriate
- DO NOT WAFFLE — keep to the question asked
- Use headings given in the questions e.g. function, composition, sources, etc. These are there to help you keep to the point. Marks will be allocated according to headings
- Where questions do not specify the number of points give five or six points
- Always include good sized clearly labelled diagrams providing important information or explanatory notes where appropriate. Check that nothing has been left out of diagrams

ON THE DAY OF THE EXAMINATION

WHEN ANSWERING THE EXAMINATION PAPER:

- Read instructions carefully
- Allocate 10 minutes to read the paper
- Carefully read and select the questions you will attempt
- Check you have the correct number of questions from the required sections
- Start with your best answer (maintains your confidence)
- Read each question before answering it, underlining key word and phrases
- Plan your answer to the question
- Allocate 25—30 minutes per question, attempt all subsections within the question
- Leave one page at the end of each question (you may want to add more)
- Move on to the next question
- WATCH THE CLOCK, time will go quickly

Finally allocate 10 minutes to recheck your answers at the end of the examination. Check written answers and diagrams. Add extra information in point form as appropriate.

PART I
SCIENTIFIC

1

THE NUTRIENTS

Nutrients are complex chemical substances found in food which are essential for a healthy body. Based on their molecular size, and quantities in which they are required by the body, nutrients are organised into two groups.

MACRO-NUTRIENTS

- Proteins
- Carbohydrates
- Lipids/fats

MICRO-NUTRIENTS

- Vitamins
- Minerals
- Water

ENERGY VALUE OF NUTRIENTS

Proteins	1 g produces 4 kcal/17 kJ
Carbohydrates	1 g produces 4 kcal/17 kJ
Lipids	1 g produces 9 kcal/37 kJ

PROTEINS

ELEMENTAL COMPOSITION OF PROTEINS

Carbon (C), Hydrogen (H), Oxygen (O), Nitrogen (N)

Sulphur (S), Iron (Fe), Phosphorus (P) and other minerals are found in some proteins.

BASIC CHEMICAL STRUCTURE OF PROTEINS

Proteins are formed from simpler, smaller building blocks called amino acids. There are 22 amino acids. Combination and number of amino acids vary with each type of protein. The basic structure of an amino acid is:

$$R - \underset{\underset{NH_2}{|}}{\overset{\overset{H}{|}}{C}} - COOH$$

Reference key:
H=hydrogen
C=carbon
R=variable
COOH=carboxyl group
NH_2=amino group

FORMATION OF PEPTIDE LINKS OR CHAINS

Amino acids join together to form polypeptide chains. Links form when a reaction takes place between the COOH (acidic carboxyl group) of one amino acid and the NH_2 (alkaline amino group) of another amino acid. The OH from the carboxyl group joins with the H from the amino group, releasing H_2O.

ESSENTIAL AND NON-ESSENTIAL AMINO ACIDS

Proteins are divided into essential and non-essential amino acids. The body cannot synthesise essential amino acids. They must be supplied in the diet. Children need 10 essential amino acids, adults require eight. Non-essential amino acids can be made in the body. The nutritional value of a protein depends on the amino acids from which it is composed.

THE ESSENTIAL AMINO ACIDS
Isoleucine, Leucine, Lysine, Methionine, Phenylalanine, Threonine, Tryptophan, Valine,
Arginine and Histidine (for children)

NON-ESSENTIAL AMINO ACIDS
Alanine, Aspartic Acid, Cysteine, Cystine, Glutamic Acid, Glycine, Proline, Serine, Tyrosine

CLASSIFICATION OF PROTEINS

Proteins may be grouped according to biological value and structure.

BIOLOGICAL VALUE

High Biological Value (HBV) or Complete proteins contain all 10 essential amino acids.
Sources: mainly from animal sources e.g. cheese, eggs, fish, meat, soya beans

Low Biological Value (LBV) or Incomplete proteins contain less of the essential amino acids.
Sources: mainly from vegetable sources e.g. cereals, pastas, potatoes, pulses

STRUCTURE OF PROTEINS

Conjugated Proteins
- Amino acids chemically combine with non-protein molecules
  Example: haemoglobin, lipoproteins

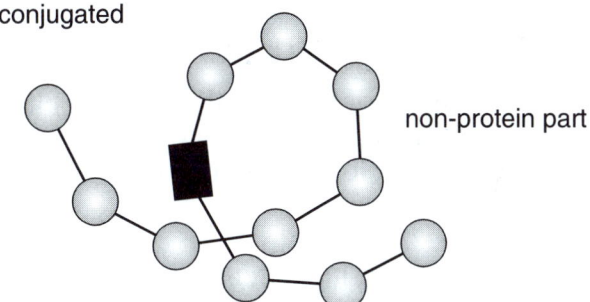

Fibrous Proteins or Structural Proteins
- Amino acid chains are organised into Coiled, Straight or Zig-zag forms
  Example: collagen, elastin, gluten

Globular Proteins or Functional proteins
- Amino acid chains are rolled around each other to form a loose ball shape
  Example: albumin

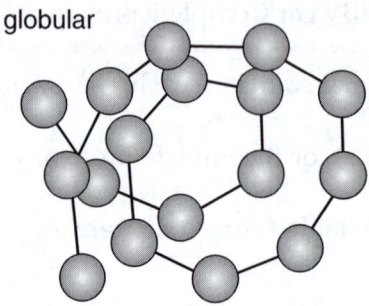

Sources of Proteins
- Animal or first class proteins (see HBV proteins)
- Vegetables or second class proteins (see LBV proteins)

COMPLEMENTARY ROLE OF PROTEINS

Some protein foods lack a few of the essential amino acids. By eating a variety of incomplete proteins the potential deficiency can be avoided. This is referred to as the complementary/supplementary role of proteins.
Example: Beans on toast

TEXTURED VEGETABLE PROTEIN (TVP)

This is a food made from soya beans. It contains all the essential amino acids and is an excellent replacement or extender for meat.

BIOLOGICAL FUNCTIONS OF PROTEINS
- Growth and repair of body cells and tissues
- Provide heat and energy (a secondary function)
- Synthesis of antibodies, enzymes and hormones

Deficiency can result in:
- Slow healing of damaged or worn cells
- Stunted growth, especially in children
- Diseases e.g. marasmus, kwashiorkor (prolonged deficiency)
- Malfunctions due to lack of hormones and enzymes
- Reduced antibodies to fight disease

GENERAL PROPERTIES OF PROTEINS

ELASTICITY
A number of fibrous proteins have elastic properties.
Example: When heat is applied during baking of breads, CO_2 expands and stretches the gluten in flour

ENZYMES
Enzymes cause coagulation of some proteins.
Examples: rennet in cheese making, rennin coagulates milk during digestion

SOLUBILITY
Most proteins are insoluble in hot or cold water. Exceptions are connective tissue and collagen, which dissolve in hot water and egg white which dissolves in cold water.

MAILLARD REACTION
Browning of food results from a chemical reaction between proteins and carbohydrates when cooking foods.
Examples: bread, pastries, roast potatoes, roast meat

EFFECTS OF HEAT ON PROTEINS

- Proteins coagulate and shrink
- Colour changes e.g. meat
- Connective tissue dissolves e.g. collagen in meat
- Denaturation may occur
- Overcooking causes protein to become indigestible

PROTEIN DEAMINATION

Amino acids not needed by the body are deaminated in the liver. This happens when:

- The amino group (NH_2) is removed from the amino acids, converted into ammonia, then urea and excreted from the body through the kidneys.
- The carboxyl group (COOH) is converted into glucose and used for heat and energy. Excess is stored in the body as glycogen and later used as an energy source.

PROTEIN DENATURATION

Denaturation occurs when the nature of a protein, i.e. shape or structure, is changed by:
- *Agitation:* beating, whipping, whisking
- *Chemicals:* acids (lemon juice, vinegar), alcohols, alkalis
- *Heat:* egg yolk, egg white, skin on milk (coagulated protein)

FOOD TESTS

BURNING TEST
Put a small sample of a protein food in a crucible, place on a tripod over a Bunsen burner. Heat gently.
Result: if a smell of burning feathers results, proteins are present

CHEMICAL OR BIURET TEST
Add some egg white or milk to a test tube. Add a few drops of potassium hydroxide and a few drops of 1% copper.
Result: protein is present, if colour changes to purple/violet

CARBOHYDRATES

ELEMENTAL COMPOSITION OF CARBOHYDRATES

Carbon (C), Hydrogen (H), Oxygen (O)
Hydrogen and oxygen are in the same proportion as water, 2:1.

CHEMICAL STRUCTURE OF CARBOHYDRATES

Basic unit of a carbohydrate is a single sugar, a monosaccharide.

GLUCOSE RING

CLASSIFICATION AND SOURCES OF CARBOHYDRATES

MONOSACCHARIDES
- Consist of simple sugars, one sugar unit
- Single chain or single ring structure
- $C_6H_{12}O_6$

Examples	Sources
Fructose	Honey
Galactose	Milk
Glucose	Fruit

DISACCHARIDES
- Consist of two monosaccharide units
- $C_{12}H_{22}O_{11}$

Examples	Composition	Sources
Lactose	Glucose + Galactose	Milk
Maltose	Glucose + Glucose	Malt
Sucrose	Glucose + Fructose	Beet and Cane Sugar

POLYSACCHARIDES
- Consist of long branching chains of monosaccharides
- $(C_6H_{10}O_5)_n$

Examples	Sources
Cellulose	Fruits, vegetables
Glycogen	Animal starch in liver and muscles
Pectin	Ripe fruits and vegetables
Starch	Cereals, root vegetables, potatoes

BIOLOGICAL FUNCTIONS OF DIGESTIBLE CARBOHYDRATES
- Source of heat and energy
- Protein sparer
- Excess stored as adipose tissue, insulates the body
- Acts as an energy store within the body

BIOLOGICAL FUNCTIONS OF INDIGESTIBLE CARBOHYDRATES
- Cellulose provides fibre in the diet, encourages peristalsis
- Cellulose prevents constipation and reduces bowel diseases

CARBOHYDRATE DEFICIENCY PROBLEMS
Deficiency diseases are rare. Problems associated with carbohydrates include:
- Obesity due to excess intake
- Dental caries/decay due to excess sugar
- Constipation and other bowel disorders

CURRENT DIETARY GUIDELINES
- Choose more dietary fibres and starches
- Reduce intake of sugars, avoid foods that are mainly sugar
- Increase intake of fruits and vegetables, use raw where possible

GENERAL PROPERTIES OF CARBOHYDRATES

Cellulose (Fibre)
- Indigestible carbohydrate
- Absorbs water but is insoluble in water
- Makes us feel full by creating bulk in the diet
- Encourages peristalsis in the digestive system
- Assists waste removal

Glycogen
- Converts to glucose, i.e. instant energy
- Dissolves in water

Pectin
- Assists the setting of preserves e.g. jams

Starch
- Forms a sticky paste when mixed with water (gelatinisation)
- Insoluble in cold water
- Starches are hygroscopic e.g. biscuits soften
- Dry heat forms dextrin e.g. toasted bread
- Dry heat causes starch grains to burst when heated and absorb fat e.g. pastry
- Moist heat causes starch to absorb moisture, burst and thicken a liquid e.g. sauce

SUGAR

- Easily digested and quickly absorbed in the body
- Sweet, crystalline substance to taste
- Soluble in water
- Some sugars remove oxygen from other substances, known as *'Reducing Sugars'*
- Hydrolysis causes complex sugars to break down into simpler molecules (*Invert Sugar*)
- Moist heat causes sugars to dissolve and become syrupy
- Further heating causes carmelisation

FOOD TESTS

TEST FOR STARCH

Place a small amount of food on a small clean dish, add a few drops of diluted iodine.
Result: a dark blue/black colour indicates starch is present

TEST FOR SUGAR

Place a small amount of food in a clean test tube. Mix equal quantities of Fehling's A and Fehling's B. A blue colour results. Using a dropper add Fehling's solution to the food and stir. Gently heat the test tube in a beaker of water over a Bunsen burner.
Result: a brick-red precipitate indicates a reducing sugar

LIPIDS

ELEMENTAL COMPOSITION OF LIPIDS

Carbon (C), Hydrogen (H) and Oxygen (O)

Lipids contain more carbon than other nutrients.

BASIC STRUCTURE/CHEMICAL STRUCTURE

The elements carbon, hydrogen and oxygen join together to form glycerol and fatty acids.

FORMATION OF A TRIGLYCERIDE (LIPID)

Glycerol is a trihydric alcohol with three OH groups. When a fatty acid combines with each of the OHs of a glycerol molecule a triglyceride is formed. During the reaction water is released.

$$\begin{array}{l} H \\ | \\ H-C-OH + \text{fatty acid} \\ | \\ H-C-OH + \text{fatty acid produces} \longrightarrow \text{Lipid} + 3H_2O \text{ (water)} \\ | \\ H-C-OH + \text{fatty acid} \\ | \\ H \end{array}$$

FATTY ACIDS

Fatty acids are divided into two groups:

SATURATED FATTY ACIDS
- Have full complement of hydrogen atoms
- Carbon atoms are joined by single bonds
- Every bond is complete, cannot hold any more hydrogen
- Solid or hard at room temperature e.g. butter, suet, lard
- Are high in cholesterol

Sources: animal e.g. animal fat, dairy products

Examples: butyric, stearic

$$\begin{array}{ccccc} O & O & O & O & O \\ \| & | & | & | & | \\ OH-C-C-C-C-C-H \\ & | & | & | & | \\ & H & H & H & H \end{array}$$

UNSATURATED FATTY ACIDS
- Are not saturated with hydrogen atoms, bonds are incomplete
- Have double bonds between two carbon atoms
- Are liquid or soft at room temperature e.g. oils
- Are low in cholesterol

Sources: fish, vegetables

Examples: monounsaturated and polyunsaturated fatty acids

Monounsaturated Fatty Acids (one double bond)
Examples: oleic acid

Polyunsaturated Fatty Acids (two or more double bonds)
Examples:
- Linoleic, two double bonds
- Linolenic, three double bonds
- Arachidonic, four double bonds

CLASSIFICATION OF LIPIDS

Lipid/fat	Source	Examples
Saturated	Animal	Dairy produce, egg yolk, meat, meat fats
Unsaturated	Vegetable	Cereals, nuts, nut oils, vegetable oils

Exceptions
- Fish liver oils are high in polyunsaturated fatty acids
- Some hard margarines have high levels of saturated fatty acids

BIOLOGICAL FUNCTIONS OF LIPIDS

- Greatest concentrated source of heat and energy
- Transport and store fat-soluble vitamins
- Insulate the body, reduce heat loss
- Protect organs e.g. kidneys
- Excess stored as adipose tissue
- Constituents of nerve sheaths and sebum
- Satiety value

EFFECTS OF LIPID DEFICIENCY

- Deficiency is rare

GENERAL PROPERTIES OF LIPIDS

- Hard or solid fats melt when heated
- Insoluble in water
- Soluble in solvents such as benzine and ether
- Form emulsions (temporary or permanent)
- Absorb flavours e.g. onions
- Degrade or become rancid
- Have limited shelf life
- Some oils can be hardened by hydrogenation

RANCIDITY

HYDROLYTIC
Caused by the action of enzymes or micro-organisms. Fatty acids and glycerol separate.

OXIDATION
Caused by oxygen combining with carbon in an unsaturated chain.

EMULSIONS

PERMANENT
An emulsifier forces a lipid and water to mix. They do not separate.

TEMPORARY
A lipid and water/liquid are mixed and when shaken together remain mixed for a short time e.g. vinegarette dressing.

EFFECTS OF HEAT ON LIPIDS

- Solid fats melt
- Melted fats and heated oils can burst into flames, give off a vapour or decompose at high temperatures. The flash and smoke points of the different fats and oils vary:

Flash point occurs in fats at 310°C and oils at 325°C
Smoke point occurs in fats at 200°C and oils at 250°C

FOOD TESTS

BROWN PAPER TEST
Press a little food on brown paper.
Result: presence of lipid is indicated by a greasy mark

SUDAN 3 DYE TEST
Add a small amount of food into a test tube. Using a dropper, pour three drops of Sudan 3 dye over the food.
Result: a pinky/red colour indicates presence of lipids

CHECKING FOR SATURATED AND UNSATURATED LIPIDS
Use two test tubes. Into test tube A put 10 g of finely chopped suet. Into test tube B put 10 ml of oil. To each add 10 ml of ether and stir. Using a clean

dropper, add iodine drop by drop to each test tube, counting the drops until a yellow colour results.
Result: saturated lipids require less iodine to produce the yellow colour than the unsaturated lipids

RECOMMENDED DIETARY ALLOWANCES

The recommended dietary allowances are referred to as the RDAs.

PROTEIN

The basic rule is 1 gram of protein per day for each kilogram of weight. Some guidelines are: child, 30–50 g; teenager, 60–80 g; adult, 55–70 g; pregnant female, 70–90 g.

CARBOHYDRATE

Fibre: 30 g per day.

LIPIDS

30–35% of total kJ intake in the diet should be supplied by lipids, half from animal and half from vegetable sources.

2

MICRO-NUTRIENTS

MINERALS

The minerals required by the body can be divided into two groups:

The **Main Minerals** are calcium, chlorine, iron, magnesium, potassium, phosphorus, sodium, sulphur.

Trace Elements, required by the body in smaller amounts, include cobalt, copper, fluorine, iodine, manganese, nickel, selenium, zinc.

CALCIUM

Food sources: dairy products (cheese, cream, milk), eggs, hard water, leafy green vegetables, tinned fish (bones) and meat

Major Functions
- Formation of strong bones and teeth
- Assists clotting of blood
- Essential for functioning of nerves and muscles

Absorption
Assisting absorption: vitamin D, phosphorus, an acid environment, protein and parathyroid hormone
Inhibiting absorption: fatty acids, oxalic acid, phytic acid and low levels of phosphorus

Deficiency can result in:
- Poor quality teeth, tooth decay
- Abnormal clotting of blood
- Osteomalacia in adults
- Osteoporosis in older people
- Rickets in children
- Nervousness, muscle cramps, pain in joints

IRON

Food sources: brown bread, green vegetables, eggs, kidney, liver, red meat

Major Functions
- Essential component of haemoglobin
- Transports oxygen to the cells
- Helps oxidation of carbohydrate

Absorption
Assisting absorption: vitamin C and protein
Inhibiting absorption: cellulose, phytic acid and oxalic acid

Deficiency can result in:
- Iron deficiency anaemia
- Fatigue, tiredness, listlessness
- Loss of appetite

PHOSPHORUS

Food sources: dairy produce, eggs, fish, green vegetables, liver, kidney

MAJOR FUNCTIONS
- Aids metabolism and energy production
- Essential for healthy bones and teeth
- Assists the absorption of calcium

EFFECTS OF DEFICIENCY
Deficiency is unlikely because phosphorus is present in most foods.

POTASSIUM

Food sources: present in most foods, good sources include cabbage, watercress, celery, parsley and courgettes

MAJOR FUNCTIONS
- Formation and functioning of body cells
- Involved in metabolism
- Promotes healthy nerves and muscles

EFFECTS OF DEFICIENCY
Deficiency is unlikely as most foods contain potassium. Severe deficiency could result in abdominal bloating, loss of appetite and muscular weakness.

IODINE

Food sources: sea fish, vegetables grown near the sea, iodised salt

MAJOR FUNCTIONS
- Essential for the production of thyroxine
- Thyroxine controls rate of metabolism

DEFICIENCY CAN RESULT IN:
- Goitre
- Tiredness
- Cretinism

SODIUM

Food sources: bacon, bread, butter, rashers, table salt

MAJOR FUNCTIONS
- Maintains water balance in body and blood
- Prevents dehydration
- Aids transmission of nerve pulses in nerve fibres

DEFICIENCY CAN RESULT IN:
- Dehydration, loss of appetite
- Low blood pressure
- Muscle cramps
- Nausea and vomiting

MAGNESIUM

Food Sources: wheat germ, brewer's yeast, cereals, nuts

MAJOR FUNCTIONS
- Aids formation of healthy bones and teeth
- Promotes healthy muscles
- Involved in energy production
- Is a co-factor in many enzymes

DEFICIENCY CAN RESULT IN:
- Muscular spasm and weakness
- Insomnia
- Reduced bone density

FLUORINE

Food sources: drinking water (tap water), sea fish, tea

MAJOR FUNCTIONS
- Aids formation of strong bones and teeth
- Is a component of tooth enamel

DEFICIENCY CAN RESULT IN:
- Poor quality bones and teeth
- Dental caries

OTHER MINERALS

Minerals	Some functions
Copper	Formation of enzymes, haemoglobin and nerve covering
Chlorine	Formation of hydrochloric acid
Selenium	Acts as an antioxidant
Zinc	Component of enzymes, boosts the immune system

MINERAL AND VITAMIN INTER-RELATIONSHIP

Mineral	What helps it work
Calcium	Vitamin D, phosphorus, magnesium
Iron	Vitamin C
Magnesium	Vitamin D, B6, calcium

The inter-relationships between folic acid, B_6, B_{12} and iron are essential for the formation of red blood cells.

VITAMINS

CLASSIFICATION

FAT-SOLUBLE VITAMINS   **WATER-SOLUBLE VITAMINS**
A or Retinol   B group
D or Calciferols   C
E or Tocopherols
K or Quinones

FAT-SOLUBLE VITAMINS

Vitamin A
Note: available in two forms, pure vitamin A (retinol) and pro-vitamin A (carotene). In the body, carotene can be converted into vitamin A.

Sources
Carotene: cabbage, carrots, dark green vegetables (kale, spinach) dried apricots, peas, prunes, tomatoes, watercress
Retinol: butter, cheese, egg yolk, fish liver oils (cod, halibut), herrings, liver, milk (summer)

Properties
- Fat-soluble vitamin, insoluble in water
- Soluble in alcohol
- Heat stable, some loss at high temperatures
- Destroyed by dehydration and long exposure to light and air

Major Functions
- Maintenance of epithelial membranes
- Prevents night blindness
- Assists the manufacture of the pigment rhodopsin in the retina
- Essential for growth and healthy skin

Deficiency can result in:
- Dry eye membranes (xerophthalmia in extreme cases)
- Dry lining membranes, dry and rough skin
- Night blindness
- Retarded growth

Watch Out for Hypervitaminosis A and D

Vitamin A and D taken in large amounts can result in toxic effects within the body. They are stored in the liver and not excreted like other vitamins. In extreme cases, an enlarged liver, diarrhoea, kidney damage, vomiting, weight loss and even death, can result.

Vitamin D: the Sunshine Vitamin
Note: available in two forms, calciferols (fish oils, action of sunshine on skin) and ergocalciferols (fungi, yeast).
Sources: action of sunlight on the skin, dairy produce (butter, cream, milk), fish liver oils (cod, halibut), oily fish (herrings), margarine

Properties
- Fat-soluble vitamin
- Insoluble in water
- Stable to acids, alkalis and heat
- Unaffected by oxidation

Functions
- Necessary for absorption and laying down of calcium and phosphorous
- Prevents rickets, a bone disease in children
- Regulates calcium balance between skeleton and bone

Deficiency can result in:
- Osteomalacia in adults
- Dental caries
- Rickets in children

Vitamin E

Food sources: most foods, cereals, eggs, margarine, meat, pulse vegetables, vegetable oils, wheat germ

Properties
- Fat-soluble vitamin, insoluble in water
- Antioxidant, protects against free oxidating radicals
- Damaged by alkalis and ultraviolet light
- Stable to heat
- Oxidised by air

Major Functions
- A powerful antioxidant in the body
- Used in food, may prevent oxidation and rancidity

Effects of Deficiency:
- None confirmed

Vitamin K

Food sources: dark green vegetables (cabbage, spinach), fish, fish liver oils, fruits (strawberries, tomatoes), liver

Properties
- Fat-soluble vitamin, insoluble in water
- Heat stable
- Destroyed by light, strong acids and alkalis

Function
- Constituent of prothrombin, essential for the clotting of the blood

Effects of Deficiency:
Blood will not clot, haemorrhaging may result

WATER-SOLUBLE VITAMINS

B GROUP VITAMINS

The main vitamins in this group are thiamine (B_1), riboflavin (B_2), pyridoxine (B_6), cyanocobalamin (B_{12}), folic acid, and nicotinic acid.

THIAMINE (B_1)
Food sources: breakfast cereals, unprocessed cereals, dairy produce (eggs, milk), fortified flour, meats (carcase meats, heart, kidney, liver, pork), vegetables, yeast, wheat germ, wholegrains, wholemeal bread

Properties
- Water-soluble vitamin
- Destroyed:
    during cooking and preservation, at high temperatures
    by dry heat
    by alkalis e.g. breadsoda
- Some loss of thiamine occurs during the milling process

Major Functions
- Aids growth in children
- Aids metabolism of carbohydrates
- Essential for functioning of nervous system
- Prevents beri-beri (disease of nervous system)
- Necessary for good health

Deficiency can result in:
- Beri-beri in severe cases
- Checked growth, poor health
- Lack of energy, tiredness and fatigue

RIBOFLAVIN (B_2)

Food sources: cheese, eggs, green vegetables (broccoli, cabbage), meats, milk, sprouting vegetables (beansprouts, bamboo shoots), yeast and yeast extract, wheat germ

Properties
- Water-soluble vitamin
- Destroyed by alkalis and ultraviolet light
- Heat stable at normal cooking temperatures
- Unstable at high temperatures

Major Functions
- Essential for growth and general health
- Aids carbohydrate and protein metabolism
- Necessary for healthy skin and eyes

Deficiency can result in:
- Checked growth and poor health
- Lack of energy, tiredness and fatigue
- Sore mouth and tongue, cracked lips
- Dermatitis
- Sensitivity to light, eye infections

PYRIDOXINE (B_6)

Food sources: most foods, cereals, fish, liver, meat, wheat germ, yeast

Properties
- Water-soluble vitamin
- Fairly stable at normal temperatures
- Sensitive to high heat, oxidation, processing, milling
- Affected by light

MAJOR FUNCTIONS
- Assists metabolism of protein, acts as a co-enzyme
- Essential for production of antibodies
- Required for growth, good health and healthy skin

Deficiency can result in:
- Anaemia, tiredness and fatigue
- Depression, irritability and nervousness
- Muscle cramps, pre-menstrual tension
- Convulsions in children

CYANOCOBALAMIN (B_{12})
Food sources: cheese, eggs, fish, liver, meats, poultry, milk, yeast

Properties
- Water-soluble vitamin
- Destroyed by strong acids and alkalis
- Heat stable to 100°C
- Sensitive to light

Functions
- Essential for healthy tissues surrounding the nerves
- Helps counteract pernicious anaemia
- Maturation of red blood cells
- Aids DNA synthesis

Deficiency can result in:
- Anxiety and irritability
- Pernicious anaemia
- Degeneration of nerve fibres

FOLIC ACID
Food sources: dark green vegetables (cabbage, broccoli, spinach), offal, pulse vegetables, wheat germ, wholegrain cereals

Properties
- Water-soluble vitamin
- Stable to acids
- Sensitive to alkalis, oxidation and light

Functions
- Essential during pregnancy
- Assists the formation of red blood cells

Deficiency can result in:
- Anaemia, during pregnancy
- Lack of energy, tiredness

NICOTINIC ACID OR NIACIN
Sources: bran, cabbage, dried fruit, fish, meat, offal, meat extracts, poultry, pulses, wheat germ, yeast. A little manufactured in the gut from tryptophan.

Properties
- Water-soluble vitamin
- Almost completely destroyed by milling
- Stable to acids, alkalis, heat and oxygen

Functions
- Assists cell respiration
- Prevents pellagra
- Necessary for growth and healthy skin

Deficiency can result in:
- Lack of energy, fatigue and weight loss
- Pellagra in severe cases
- Tension and irritability

Deficiency is rare.

VITAMIN C (ALSO KNOWN AS ASCORBIC ACID)
Food sources: fresh fruits and vegetables e.g. blackcurrants, citrus fruits, strawberries, peppers, parsley, broccoli, cabbage, potatoes

Properties
- Water-soluble vitamin, destroyed by steeping
- Destroyed by alkalis i.e. bicarbonate of soda
- Destroyed during cooking
- Destroyed by oxidation (peeling, chopping, slicing, shredding)
- Reduced during food processing

Functions
- Acts as an antioxidant
- Assists the healing of cuts and wounds
- Builds strong bones and teeth
- Essential for the absorption of iron
- Helps prevent infections, colds and flu
- Necessary for formation of collagen
- Prevents scurvy

Deficiency can result in:
- Slow healing of cuts and wounds
- Infections e.g. bleeding gums
- Poor absorption of iron, resulting in anaemia
- Scurvy
- Weakening of blood vessel walls

Food Test for Vitamin C: The DC PIP Test

Into a clean dry test tube place 1 DC PIP (dichlorophenol indophenol) tablet with 15 cm^3 water. Stir together until a blue solution results. Using a dropper gradually add drops of fruit juice (orange, lemon).

Result: vitamin C is present if the mixture turns from blue to pink and eventually to a clear liquid.

RETAINING THE MAXIMUM VITAMINS AND MINERALS

When using fruit and vegetables:
- Avoid cooking or reheating, eat raw if possible
- Avoid peeling, eat the skin where possible
- Use a sharp knife when peeling or shredding fruits and vegetables
- Never soak for long periods of time or overnight
- Never add breadsoda when cooking cabbage, destroys vitamin C
- Cook for shortest time in smallest amount of liquid with a lid on the saucepan
- Prepare and cook just before serving, serve at once
- Use leftover cooking liquids for casseroles, sauces and soups

RECOMMENDED DIETARY ALLOWANCES (RDAs)

MINERALS

Calcium: teenagers 1200 mg, adults 800 mg, pregnancy/nursing 1200 mg
Iron: children 15 mg, adults 10–15 mg, pregnancy/nursing 15–20 mg
Phosphorus: none (widely found in food)
Iodine: 150 μg
Sodium: 2 g
Potassium: none
Fluorine: 2 mg

VITAMINS

Vitamin A: children 300 μg, adults 700 μg, pregnancy 1200 μg
Vitamin D: children, pregnancy/nursing 10 μg, adults 2.5 μg
Vitamin E: none given (widely available)
Vitamin K: none given (widely available)
Vitamin B group: Thiamine: 0.8–1 mg
   Riboflavin: 1–1.5 mg
   Niacin: 12–17 mg
   Pyridoxine: 2 mg
   Folic acid: children/adults 200 μg
      pregnancy/nursing 300–400 μg
   Cyanocobalamin: 1.5 μg
Vitamin C: 40 mg

WATER

ELEMENTAL COMPOSITION

2 hydrogen + 1 oxygen = H_2O (ratio 2:1)

GENERAL PROPERTIES

- Found in three states, ice (below 0°C), liquid (0–100°C), steam (over 100°C)
- Lacks colour, smell and taste
- Neutral pH value (pH 7)
- Substances dissolve readily in water

MAIN FUNCTIONS
- Assists digestion and absorption of food (metabolism)
- Constituent of cells, body fluids and tissues
- Transports carbon dioxide, oxygen, nutrients, enzymes and hormones
- Source of calcium and fluorine
- Removes waste from the body
- Regulates body temperature
- Refreshing to drink, quenches thirst

SOURCES

Water is found in most foods, alcohol, beverages (milk, tea) drinking water, fruits and vegetables.

DAIRY REQUIREMENTS

A recommended minimum intake of 2–2.5 litres.

FLUORIDATION OF WATER

Water leaving the reservoir may be treated by fluoridation by the Local Authority. This helps to strengthen teeth.

3

ADDITIVES, ENZYMES AND THE COLOUR AND FLAVOUR OF FOOD

ADDITIVES

Additives are chemical or natural ingredients added to food. Some additives are referenced by E numbers. Additives are added to:
- Improve colour, flavour and texture
- Increase or improve shelf-life of food

- Increase range of food available
- Prevent oxidation
- Reduce and inhibit action of enzymes and micro-organisms
- Supplement nutrients in food (fortified)

DISADVANTAGES MIGHT INCLUDE:
- Interference with the natural life cycle of food
- Side effects e.g. allergic reactions
- Digestive reactions
- Some colours look unnatural

CLASSIFICATION OF ADDITIVES
- Colourings
- Flavourings
- Nutritive Additives or Supplements
- Physical Conditioning Agents
- Preservatives

COLOURINGS
Colourings are used to:
- Respond to consumer demand for foods with good colours
- Improve the natural colour of food
- Improve the colour of preserved food (jams, jellies)

Examples of Colourings
Natural: Annatto, caramel, chlorophyll, cochineal, saffron
Synthetic: red, riboflavin (yellow), tartrazine

Examples of Uses
Beverages (soft drinks), cakes, convenience foods (sauces), ice cream, jelly, preserves (canned foods, jams, jellies), sweets

FLAVOURINGS
Flavourings are used to enhance the natural flavours of food

Examples of Flavourings
Flavour enhancers: monosodium glutamate
Natural: alcohol, citric acid, essences, seasoning, spices, sugar
Synthetic sweeteners: saccharine, sorbitol

NUTRITIVE ADDITIVES OR SUPPLEMENTS
Nutritive additives are used to:
- Enhance the nutritive value of foods
- Replace nutrients lost during the manufacturing process

Examples of Uses
Found in breakfast cereals, flour, fruit juices and margarine

PHYSICAL CONDITIONING AGENTS

Main Agents	What they do
Anti-caking agents	Prevent lumps forming in foods Uses: icing sugar, powdered milk, salt
Antioxidants:	Prevent oxidation and rancidity Uses: biscuits, cooking oils, crisps
Bulking agents:	Add to the bulk of the food but not to the energy value
Emulsifiers:	Stabilise the consistency of some foods Uses: desserts, salad dressings, ice cream, mayonnaise
Glazing agents:	Give a shiny appearance to food, seal food and prevent it drying out Uses: chewing gum, citrus fruit, dried fruit, sweets
Stabilizers:	Prevent substances from separating
Thickeners:	Add to the viscosity of food Uses: packet sauces and soups

Other additives include: anti-spattering agents, buffers, gelling agents, humectants, modified starch, packaging gas, release agents, solvents and vitamins

PRESERVATIVES
Reasons for Using Preservatives
- To inhibit growth of enzymes and micro-organisms
- To increase variety of foods available out of season
- To increase the shelf-life of food
- To reduce waste by preserving food for use out of season
- To prevent oxidation of certain foods

Classification of preservatives
Natural: Alcohol, salt, spices, sugar, vinegar, wood smoke
Chemical: Benzoic acid, potassium nitrate, sodium nitrate, sulphur dioxide
Examples of Uses: found in cakes, chutneys, coffee, convenience foods (bacon products, sausages), cured meats, flour, fruit juices, jams, jellies, pickles, processed foods, yoghurts

ANTIOXIDANTS

Antioxidants are substances that inactivate highly reactive and destructive chemical substances called 'free radicals'. Free radicals are a by-product of the body's metabolism and are essential, in measured amounts, but excess can be harmful in the body. Beta-carotene, vitamins C and E are examples of antioxidants.

ENZYMES AND CO-ENZYMES

ENZYMES
Enzymes are organic catalysts (protein in nature) that are involved in chemical reactions but remain unchanged themselves.

GENERAL PROPERTIES
- Each has only one function (reaction specific)
- To function some enzymes require a co-enzyme
- pH sensitive, enzymes have specific requirements
- Remain unchanged after the chemical reaction
- Sensitive to temperature, each enzyme has a specific temperature range
- Low temperatures inactivate enzymes, high temperatures destroy them

GENERAL FUNCTIONS
- Aid cellular respiration and excretion
- Involved in fermentation and food spoilage
- Involved in the natural life cycle of food

CO-ENZYMES

These are the non-protein part of some enzymes which are required by the enzyme to function.

CHEMICAL AND PHYSICAL ASPECTS OF COLOUR AND FLAVOUR

CHEMICAL ASPECTS OF COLOUR

COLOURS OF FOODS ARE DETERMINED BY:
- Natural pigments e.g. betalaines, carotene, chlorophyll, tannin
- Action of enzymes e.g. maturation process
- Oxidation e.g. fruits going brown
- Diet of an animal e.g. grass and commercial feeds for beef, pigs, poultry
- Effects of cooking e.g. carmelisation, Maillard reaction, oxidation

PHYSICAL ASPECTS OF COLOUR

The reactions brought about by our visual senses to food colour determines if a food is appetising. The physical colour:
- Indicates freshness, maturity and quality of a food
- Influences the visual senses
- Encourages people to buy food e.g. vibrant bright colours

CHEMICAL ASPECTS OF FLAVOUR

The chemical aspects of flavour are determined by:
- Chemical composition of foods causing sweet, salty, sour and bitter flavours
- Added flavours, essences and spices made from dried barks, roots, seeds
- Use of essential plant oils
- Blending of flavours during preparation and cooking of food

PHYSICAL ASPECTS OF FLAVOUR

The physical aspects of flavour are determined by:
- Sense of *Taste*: taste buds in the tongue are sensitive to four tastes: sweet, salt, sour and bitter

- Sense of *Smell*: aroma or food smells stimulate the digestive juices and saliva production

Taste and smell work as physical indicators of flavour and together stimulate the taste buds.

4

PLANNING BALANCED DIETS

A healthy balanced diet contains nutrients, in the correct proportions, for use within the body. Foods are organised into different food groups. A balanced diet must cater for differences in activity, age, growth and special dietary requirements.

THE FOOD GROUPS

Food Groups	Number of Servings per Day	Main Dietary Value
Cereal/bread/potato	Adults 6 Children 4	B group vitamins Main energy source, fibre
Fruit/vegetable	4+	Fibre, minerals, vitamins, water
Milk/cheese	Adults/children 3 Adolescents 4 Pregnancy/nursing 5	Calcium, protein, lipid Vitamins A and B group
Protein (Meat/Meat Alternatives)	Adults/children 2 Pregnancy 3	Protein, B group vitamins Iron, other minerals
Others	None given	Eat sparingly, empty kilocalories

LATEST HEALTHY EATING GUIDELINES

IN ALL DIETS

- Eat a variety of foods, choosing recommended servings from different food groups
- Increase intake of fibre-rich foods
- Reduce intake of saturated fats, salt and sugar

IN THE DIET OF ADOLESCENT GIRLS AND WOMEN

- Increase intake of calcium and iron-rich foods

SUMMARY OF DIETARY REQUIREMENTS

BABIES

The early stages of life are a period of rapid growth. Breast feeding is recommended. Breast milk contains nutrients, in the correct proportions, at right temperature. Strictly follow the instructions with formula milk, do not over- or under-dilute. Begin to supplement milk with other foods as the baby gets older. Babies are born with a supply of iron to last a few months. Begin to supplement with iron-rich foods after a few months.

INCLUDE

- During weaning, a more varied diet e.g. puréed fruits, soups, vegetables
- Sieved/puréed meat, fish, egg yolk e.g. for protein
- Puréed vegetables and fresh fruits to supply minerals and vitamins
- At about 4–6 months introduce iron-rich and vitamin C-rich foods
- Between 6 months and 1 year, more solid foods (mashed, small pieces) e.g. breakfast cereals, bread, fruit, pasta, rice, poultry, fish, grated cheese
- Starchy carbohydrates will provide energy

EXCLUDE

- Fatty, fried and spicy foods, salt and sugar

CHILDREN

Children need excellent supplies of foods for growth and energy. A varied balanced diet with foods from all the food groups is recommended. Children should eat at regular mealtimes without rushing. Provide healthy snacks between meals e.g. fresh fruit, yoghurt. Avoid the development of 'faddy' eating habits. Encourage a healthy balanced diet from the beginning. Serve attractively presented small portions to children rather than large adult portions. Foods should be served in easy to manage portions.

INCLUDE
- Protein foods for growth and repair e.g. cheese, eggs, fish and meat
- Starchy carbohydrates for energy e.g. wholegrain breads, potatoes, pasta
- Carbohydrates in vegetables will supply fibre or roughage
- Carbohydrates and fats for energy
- Calcium and vitamin D for healthy bones and teeth
- Vitamins A, C and iron
- Minerals and vitamins to protect against disease e.g. fruits and vegetables

ADOLESCENTS/TEENAGERS

Adolescence is a time of rapid growth and increased activity. Teenagers should avoid snacking on 'empty kilocalorie' foods between meals: fast foods, fatty foods, chocolates, pastries and sweets. Healthy snacks e.g. fresh fruit, wholemeal sandwiches, are recommended instead of bars and biscuits. Include milk and cheese in their diet. Encourage teenagers to eat regular meals, especially healthy breakfasts. Packed lunches should be taken to school.

INCLUDE
- Foods from the food groups as recommended
- Protein foods (milk and cheese) for rapid growth and repair
- Good supply of energy foods e.g. whole cereals, pasta, potatoes
- High-fibre foods (cereals, fruit), prevent constipation and bowel diseases
- Calcium- and vitamin D-rich foods for strong bones and teeth
- Extra calcium and iron foods (cabbage, broccoli) for adolescent girls
- Mineral and vitamins to protect against disease, fruits and vegetables
- Water and fresh fruit juices for healthy systems and skin

ADULTS

The rate of growth slows down in adulthood. Cells are constantly being replaced, protein is needed for this activity. Body size and type of activities determine the amount of energy required e.g. sedentary or manual work, sporting activities. Energy intake must balance energy output.

It is recommended that adults reduce their intake of salt, saturated fats, sugars and alcohol (empty kilocalories). Women need extra calcium to protect against osteoporosis and increased iron to reduce incidents of anaemia. Low-fat foods are suitable for people suffering from obesity and heart disease. Manual workers require extra energy foods and vitamin B.

INCLUDE
- Balance of animal and vegetable protein e.g. fish, poultry, pulses
- Plenty of high-fibre food e.g. potatoes, vegetables, whole cereals
- For women, calcium and iron-rich foods e.g. green leafy vegetables, cheese
- Minerals and vitamins for general good health e.g. fruits and vegetables
- Adequate supply of vitamins A, C and E (antioxidants)
- Calcium and vitamin D to prevent osteoporosis
- Plenty of water and fruit juices

PREGNANT/NURSING MOTHERS

Nutritional needs increase during pregnancy. The developing baby relies on the mother for all nutritional requirements. A well-balanced varied concentrated diet is essential for mother and baby.

AVOID
- Fried, spicy, sugary foods, alcohol, coffee and tea
- Eggs just barely cooked, danger of *Salmonella*
- Cook–chill products and unpasteurised cheeses, danger of *Listeria*

INCLUDE
- Concentrated proteins for growth of the foetus
- Starchy carbohydrates for energy e.g. whole cereals, potatoes, pasta
- High-fibre foods to prevent constipation e.g. fruits, vegetables, whole cereals
- Calcium and vitamin D for development of healthy bones and teeth in the baby
- Iron for healthy blood aided by vitamin C e.g. leafy green vegetables

- Other minerals and vitamins for protection against disease
- Plenty of fruit juices and water
- Folic acid before and during pregnancy, follow doctor's advice

THE ELDERLY

Factors influencing foods that the elderly buy and the methods of cooking include change in energy requirements, reduced income, poor general health e.g. dental problems, poor eyesight and, frequently, difficulties in shopping. Sometimes elderly people are less mobile.

GENERALLY
- Foods should be easy to prepare and cook
- Serve smaller portions and more frequent meals
- Choose foods that are easy to chew and digest
- Choose easy to digest proteins e.g. fish, poultry
- Reduce intake of high cholesterol foods and sugars
- Reduce salt intake to prevent high blood pressure
- Balance energy intake with energy expended

INCLUDE
- Concentrated protein foods for growth and repair of worn cells
- Starchy carbohydrates for energy
- Dietary fibre to help avoid constipation
- Calcium- and vitamin D-rich foods to prevent osteoporosis
- Iron and vitamin C for healthy blood, to prevent anaemia
- Low-fat dairy foods for calcium, vitamins A and D
- Minerals and vitamins to prevent disease and infections e.g. fruits and vegetables

INVALIDS AND CONVALESCENTS

Follow doctor's orders regarding diet during illness. Energy levels reduce during illness but increase during recovery. Include easy-to-digest protein and low energy foods. Use fresh, high quality foods, serve in small portions. Choose light cooking methods e.g. steaming and poaching. Avoid cream cakes, fatty and spiced foods. Never use reheated foods in the invalid diet.

INCLUDE
- Concentrated easy-to-digest protein foods
- Low energy foods

- Vitamin C and iron to assist recovery and healing
- Minerals and vitamins to fight infection and aid recovery
- Diluted fruit juices and water to prevent dehydration

SPECIAL DIETS

COELIAC

Individuals who are unable to break down gluten, the protein found in wheat and some other cereals, are called coeliacs. Proteins are broken down into amino acids, but in the case of gluten, it remains in a large molecule. When absorbed, these molecules damage the lining of the small intestine. This results in an inability to absorb other nutrients effectively. Anaemia, diarrhoea and reduced body weight may result.

GENERAL DIETARY RECOMMENDATIONS
- Stick to a gluten-free diet
- Always read the labels on foods, look for the gluten-free symbol
- Avoid batter, some breakfast cereals, bread, packet sauces, sausages, soups, pasta, stuffings, foods coated with breadcrumbs (check food labels)

Suitable foods: cornflour, dairy products, gluten-free flour, popcorn, rice, rice products (rice cakes), soya products, meat and fish (uncoated), fruits and vegetables

DIABETES

TYPE 1: INSULIN-DEPENDENT DIABETES

Insulin-dependent diabetes occurs when the pancreas does not manufacture insulin to control the sugar levels in the blood. Little glucose remains in the body for energy as it is excreted by the kidneys. Treatment involves insulin injections.

TYPE 2: NON-INSULIN-DEPENDENT DIABETES

This type of diabetes can occur in older people and is associated with obesity. The pancreas produces insulin but the insulin fails to function. The glucose remains in the bloodstream and is not available to the cells. Treatment involves a change in diet.

General Dietary Recommendations
- Follow the doctor's recommended dietary programme
- Never miss meals or snacks, eat regularly
- Eat fibre-rich foods
- Avoid sugary foods and drinks
- Balance dietary programme with a healthy lifestyle to include regular exercise
- Always check the labels on food as to suitability for diabetics

VEGETARIANS

Vegetarians do not eat fish and meat, or in some cases animal products, for a variety of reasons e.g. cultural, health, moral, religious. There are two types: lacto-vegetarians and vegans. Vegetarians rarely suffer from bowel problems, heart disease, high blood pressure or obesity.

A vegetarian diet is high in fibre and low in fat. The main food groups used by vegetarians when planning their diet are beans and nuts, fruit and vegetables and grains.

Lacto-vegetarians
Lacto-vegetarians do not eat fish, meat or poultry, but include some foods of animal origin e.g. cheese, eggs, milk, yoghurt. Cereals, fruit, nuts and vegetables are important in their diet. Planning a diet for a lacto-vegetarian is easy because of the wide range of foods that they choose to eat.

Vegans
Vegans live completely on vegetables. The diet of a vegan is very strict. Because of the absence of animal foods, a vegan diet could lack calcium, iron and vitamin B_{12}. Vegans must take a vitamin B supplement. Their diet has to be well planned to ensure that all the nutrients are present, in the correct proportions, for a balanced diet.

General Guidelines or Key Points to Consider
- Read labels on all convenience foods for hidden animal products
- For vegans choose protein foods such as pulses, cereals, nuts, soya products
- Replace meat with soya protein, textured vegetable protein
- For lacto-vegetarians choose protein foods such as cheese, eggs, milk
- Choose high fibre-rich foods e.g. breads, cereals, fruits, vegetables, potatoes

- Use vegetable stocks for vegetarian casseroles, soups and stews
- Sources of vitamin B include whole cereals, pulse vegetables and yeast extracts
- Include calcium- and iron-rich foods from plant sources
- Use vegetable fats and oils to replace butter and margarines

HIGH FIBRE DIET

Dietary fibre is composed of cellulose, lignin and pectin. Its main function in the diet is to absorb water, make the waste in the bowel bulky and stimulate the walls of the intestines to produce wave-like movements called peristalsis. Cereals, grains, fruits and vegetables are excellent sources of fibre. Refining foods reduces the fibre content.

BENEFITS OF A HIGH FIBRE DIET
- Prevents constipation, heart disease and gallstones
- May also reduce bowel diseases
- Useful for weight-reducing diets
- Provides more bulk than starch or sugar

GUIDELINES/RECOMMENDATIONS
- Replace refined foods with fresh whole varieties e.g. brown rice
- Include pulse vegetables, good sources of dietary fibre
- Choose whole cereals e.g. wholewheat pasta, muesli, porridge
- Use salads, chopped nuts, dried fruits and fresh fruits
- Eat plenty of fresh fruits and vegetables

OBESITY

When a person's body weight is 20% above the recommended weight for their height, they are considered obese or overweight. The main cause of obesity is that energy intake is greater than energy output.

HEALTH PROBLEMS ASSOCIATED WITH OBESITY
- Diabetes, difficulties in childbirth, heart disease, infertility, joint problems, respiratory difficulties and varicose veins

GENERAL RECOMMENDATIONS
- Consult a doctor before starting a weight-reducing diet
- Balance a weight-reducing diet with an exercise programme

PLANNING BALANCED DIETS

- Reduce intake of sugars and fats e.g. biscuits, cakes, etc.
- Do not cook foods in saturated animal fats
- Eat high fibre carbohydrates for dietary fibre e.g. whole cereals
- Raw fruit and vegetables will provide vitamins and minerals
- Do not reduce protein intake, choose lean meats, poultry, white fish
- Drink plenty of water, reduce alcohol intake

CORONARY HEART DISEASE

Due to a build up of the waxy substance, called cholesterol, the flow of blood through the coronary arteries may slow down. Blood pressure rises, arteries become blocked and a heart attack could result. Low-fat diets are recommended for people suffering from heart disease or for those at risk of developing heart disease in the future.

General Recommendations
- Follow the doctor's guidelines
- Choose a low-fat diet
- Balance intake of saturated animal fats with unsaturated fats
- Reduce salt and sugars in food preparation and cooking
- Choose cooking methods that do not use fat e.g. grilling, poaching
- Avoid alcohol, stop smoking
- Balance work, exercise, home life, social life and manage stress

ANAEMIA

Anaemia may result from a lack of iron in the diet, malabsorption of iron in the body, heavy blood losses or pernicious anaemia. Reasons for anaemia are:

Deficiency of iron in the diet: eat iron-rich green leafy vegetables, eggs, red meat, liver, kidney and whole cereals.

Malabsorption of iron in the body: include plenty of vitamin C, fruits and vegetables. This assists the absorption of iron.

Heavy blood losses e.g. menstruation: eat an iron-rich diet.

Pernicious anaemia: the intrinsic factor, which affects the absorption of vitamin B_{12}, is missing in gastric juice. Take vitamin B_{12} supplements and eat liver.

GASTRIC AND DUODENAL ULCERS

Gastric ulcers develop in the stomach, duodenal ulcers at the beginning of the duodenum.

Mucous membranes can become inflamed, an open sore develops which can perforate the organ wall. Hydrochloric acid and pepsin cause ulcers to be painful. Ulcers may result from, or be aggravated by, alcohol, drugs, hereditary factors, stress and smoking.

GENERAL RECOMMENDATIONS
- Avoid alcohol, caffeine, fried and spicy foods
- Develop a more balanced lifestyle, less stressful
- Eat regularly, do not snack between meals
- Take time to have relaxed meals, do not rush
- Stop smoking, reduce alcohol consumption

GALLSTONES

Cholesterol and bile salts build up into hard deposits in the gall bladder. If large stones develop they can block the bile duct and cause pain. Stones are sometimes removed by laser treatment or surgery. Choose a low-fat diet to reduce the development of gallstones

ACNE

During adolescence, the increased production of sebum frequently results in a skin condition called acne. Skin pores, blocked by the sebum, form blackheads, become infected and develop into pimples. A healthy balanced diet is recommended with lots of fresh fruit, vegetables, fruit juices, water and a low intake of fats. Avoid fried and snack foods.

GASTRO-ENTERITIS AND DIARRHOEA

When the intestinal and stomach walls become inflamed and are affected by micro-organisms the condition is called gastro-enteritis. Symptoms include cramps, pain, nausea, vomiting and diarrhoea. If fluid intake is not increased dehydration could occur.

GENERAL RECOMMENDATIONS
- Get doctor if the symptoms are severe
- Check if it is contagious and follow doctor's advice
- Increase fluid intake, do not eat for 24 hours
- Introduce easily digested light foods slowly

EATING DISORDERS

Eating disorders affect young women and, increasingly, young men. Individuals suffering from such disorders want to remain thin and have a distorted image of their body shape and weight. Eating disorders are complex conditions that require professional help.

ANOREXIA NERVOSA
The fear of becoming fat is accompanied by some or all of the following: abuse of laxatives, over-exercising, self-induced vomiting and starvation.

BULIMIA NERVOSA
The fear of becoming fat sometimes results in individuals over-eating or binge eating, and then vomiting to remove food from their system so that they do not gain weight.

5

NUTRITION OF FOOD

MEAT

CLASSIFICATION

Carcase meat: cattle (beef, veal), sheep (lamb, mutton), pig (pork, bacon, ham)
Game: duck, hare, rabbit, pheasant, venison (protected by law)
Offal: internal organs of animals e.g. kidneys, liver, heart
Poultry: domesticated birds e.g. chicken (broiler, poussin), duck, goose, turkey

NUTRITIVE VALUE

Proteins: excellent source of HBV proteins
Carbohydrates: none present, traces of glycogen in liver
Lipids: visible and invisible saturated fats
Minerals: iron (excellent source), calcium, phosphorous, sulphur
Vitamins: B group, fat-soluble vitamins A and D
Water: 60–70%

DIETETIC VALUE

Meat provides an excellent supply of HBV protein e.g. collagen, elastin, globulin and myosin. Meat is an important source of iron and B group vitamins (red meat, offal). Minerals are present in most meats. Meat lacks vitamin C and carbohydrates. For this reason combine meat with high fibre starchy foods e.g. potatoes and salads. Meat provides fat-soluble vitamins A and D. The amount of fat present varies with age, size, type and cut of meat. Choose leaner cuts of meat to reduce intake of saturated animal fats. Choose low-fat cooking methods e.g. grilling rather than frying. Cooked meat contains less water than uncooked meat.

THE STRUCTURE OF MEAT

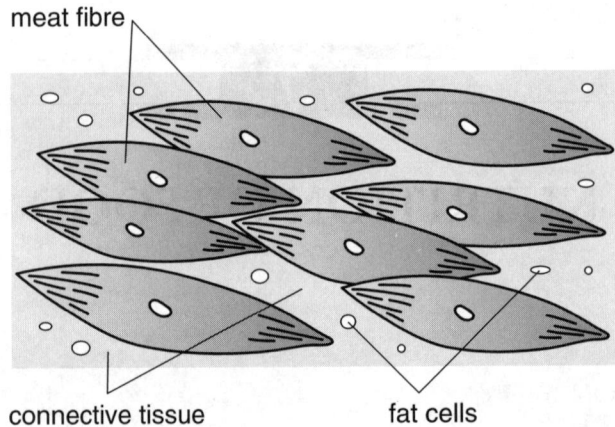

Meat is composed of bundles of long and short muscle fibres containing walls of elastin, nuclei, and proteins, and juices containing extractives, minerals and proteins. Fat is present between the fibres as adipose tissue and on outer surfaces of organs e.g. kidneys.

TOUGHNESS OR TENDERNESS OF MEAT

This depends on:
- Activity of animal e.g. less active animal is more tender
- Age of animal e.g. younger animal is more tender
- Hanging of meat:
    rigor mortis develops, lactic acid develops, meat becomes more tender
- Treatment of animal before and after slaughter

- Cooking method/s selected:
    long slow methods tenderise cheaper, tougher cuts of meat
    short cooking methods for expensive, tender cuts of meat

MEAT IS TENDERISED BY:
- Using chemical tenderisers before slaughter or prior to cooking
- Hanging meat for the correct period of time
- Beating meat with a steak hammer
- Marinading meat, prior to cooking, to break down the fibres
- Mincing meat or cutting it into small cubes
- Selecting slow moist methods of cooking for tougher meat

EFFECTS OF HEAT/COOKING ON MEAT:
- Micro-organisms are destroyed e.g. bacteria
- Collagen changes to gelatin, meat becomes tender
- Proteins coagulate, surfaces are sealed, meat becomes firmer and shrinks
- Some B group vitamins are destroyed
- Fats melt, providing moisture and adding to the flavour
- Colour of meat changes from red to brown
- Extractives are released, flavour and smell develop

CHOOSING MEAT

When choosing meat ensure that:
- It has been hung correctly
- Cuts suit the dish being cooked
- Cuts are firm and moist
- It is lean, has little bone, fat and gristle

BUYING MEAT

Buy from a reputable butcher's shop or supermarket where:
- Surfaces and equipment are spotlessly clean and hygienic
- Shop is well ventilated with bright surfaces
- Assistants do not handle money and meat: cross-contamination
- Assistants have hair covered and wear protective clothing
- Raw and cooked meats are stored and handled separately
- Plastic gloves are worn by the assistants handling meat
- Buy meat in small quantities unless freezing
- Buy frozen meat from a reliable source

STORING MEAT
- Check use-by-dates, use fresh meat within 2 days of purchase
- Remove wrapping, place on clean plate, cover with clingfilm and store in fridge
- Store raw and cooked meats <u>separately</u> in the fridge, never on same plate or shelf

USING MEAT
- Remove wrapper and prepare as required
- Always thaw frozen meat fully
- Use separate chopping boards for raw and cooked meats
- Cook meats thoroughly to destroy the micro-organisms
- Cool meats quickly, cover loosely and store in fridge

POULTRY

CLASSIFICATION
Domestic: chicken, duck, goose, turkey, ostrich
Game: duck, pheasant

NUTRITIVE VALUE
Proteins: good source of high biological value protein
Carbohydrates: none in poultry
Lipids: little fat, lower than red meat
Minerals: calcium, iron
Vitamins: B group
Water: varies (depends on type and method of processing)

DIETETIC VALUE
As most of the fat is located just inside the skin, poultry has a lower fat content than red meat. It is a good alternative to meat when trying to reduce saturated fats in the diet, for invalids and the elderly. As poultry has no carbohydrates and is low in minerals and vitamins, serve it with foods rich in these nutrients e.g. pastas, potatoes, vegetables and salads. Poultry is an easily digested food.

BUYING POULTRY
- Buy from a reliable, hygienic shop or supermarket
- If prepacked always check the 'use by' label
- Do not buy poultry that has a bad smell and a poor colour

- Ensure that frozen poultry is frozen 'solid'
- Frozen poultry should have undamaged wrappers
- Never buy frozen poultry that has begun to thaw or if the wrapper is torn

Characteristics of Poultry

Good poultry will be fresh, have a characteristic smell and a plump, pliable breastbone.

Using Poultry

- Wash hands thoroughly before and after handling raw poultry
- Wash chopping board and knives to prevent cross-contamination
- Remove from wrapper and remove giblets
- Place on clean plate, cover loosely, store in fridge
- Store frozen poultry in the freezer immediately
- Thaw frozen poultry thoroughly before using it
- Cook stuffing separately
- Cook poultry thoroughly to destroy all bacteria
- Remove from oven, place on clean dishes or plates
- Cool leftover poultry quickly, cover and store in the fridge
- Use up quickly, never reheat poultry remaining on the carcase

FISH

Fish may be classified according to nutritional content, shape and habitat.

NUTRITIONAL CONTENT AND EXAMPLES

White fish	Oily fish	Shellfish
Cod	Herring	Crab
Haddock	Mackerel	Oysters
Plaice	Salmon	Prawns
Whiting	Trout	Mussels

SHAPE

Flat e.g. plaice, sole
Round e.g. salmon, trout

HABITAT OR SOURCE

Freshwater fish: found in rivers and lakes e.g. perch, pike, trout
Saltwater fish: there are two groups:
    Demersal: fish that swim on the seabed e.g. plaice, sole
    Pelagic: fish that swim near the surface e.g. herring, mackerel

NUTRITIVE VALUE

Proteins: HBV protein, not quite as much as in meat
Carbohydrate: none present
Lipids: high in polyunsaturated fats/oils, a little fat found in shellfish
Minerals: phosphorus, potassium, calcium. Sea fish provide iodine
Vitamins: fat-soluble vitamins A and D in oily fish and fish liver oils, B group vitamins
Water: ranges from 65% in oily fish, 75% in shellfish to 80% in white fish

DIETETIC VALUE

Fish, like poultry, is a good alternative to meat as it supplies high biological value protein. It is high in polyunsaturated fatty acids. In white fish fat is found in the liver. In oily fish fat is distributed in the flesh. White fish is easier to digest than oily fish. Fish should be included in the diets of elderly people, invalids and those on low cholesterol diets. Oily fish provides valuable fat-soluble vitamins. All fish supply B group vitamins. Fish is a good source of minerals in the diet, particularly iodine. Fish bones contain calcium e.g. tinned fish, bones are soft enough to be eaten. Fish does not contain iron. Serve fish with carbohydrate-, vitamin C- and iron-rich foods.

STRUCTURE OF FISH

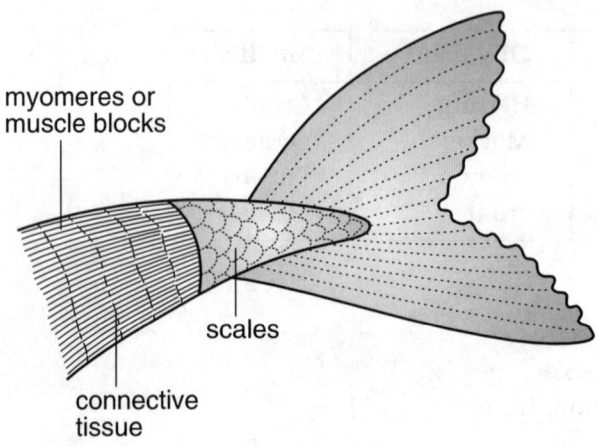

Fish is composed of bundles of fibres, myomeres, containing extractives, proteins and water. Myomeres are held together by a connective tissue called collagen, which changes to gelatin when fish is cooked. The outside skin of fish is composed of scales. Fibres in shellfish are coarser and the fish is covered by a hard protective shell.

CUTS OF FISH

- Cutlet, fillets, steak, tailpiece

STALING OF FISH

Once caught, fish struggle and use up their energy stores of glycogen. Lactic acid (which would preserve the fish) is not formed, fish stales quickly and begins to 'go off' producing tri-methylamine. Because of this, fish must be processed almost as soon as it is caught.

EFFECTS OF COOKING ON FISH

- Micro-organisms and parasites are destroyed
- Collagen changes to gelatin
- Colour changes from transparent to opaque
- Protein coagulates, fish shrinks
- Overcooking causes flakes to fall apart
- Minerals and vitamins dissolve into the cooking liquid
- Some loss of B group vitamins

SHOPPING FOR FISH

Choose fish:
- When in season when it is cheapest, medium size are best
- With bright, fresh looking bulging eyes, firm flesh, bright red gills and a scaly outer skin
- That smells of fresh fish and not that of stale fish
- In cutlets, fillets, steaks or whole with firm flesh

Buy from a reliable clean fishmonger, shop or supermarket. Choose shellfish with tightly shut, undamaged shells. Check wrappers on pre-packed fish and sell by date. Ensure that frozen fish is frozen solid.

STORING FISH

- Remove wrapping, place on clean dish, cover and place in the fridge
- Store away from other foods

- Use on the same day of purchase
- Put frozen fish into the freezer to prevent it thawing out

COMMERCIAL PROCESSING OF FISH

Because it decays rapidly, fish must be processed quickly after catching it. Processing takes place on board large factory ships and in land-based processing factories.

Methods, Examples and Effects of Processing

Canning
Crab, herrings, sardines, salmon and tuna in brine, oil or sauces. A little loss of B group vitamins. Increased calcium because the bones are processed and can be eaten.

Freezing
All types of fish in cutlets, steaks, pre-prepared dishes, fish cakes, fish fingers, plain or in sauces. The action of bacteria and parasites is inhibited. The nutritive value is almost the same as when fresh. A little loss of B group vitamin. Fish is blast frozen at –30°C.

Smoking
Can be done naturally in a kiln over oak chips or artificially dyed and flavoured. Micro-organisms e.g. bacteria are destroyed, fish changes to an orange colour and has a smoky flavour. Cold smoking at 30°C; hot smoking at 110°C.

EGGS

STRUCTURE OF AN EGG

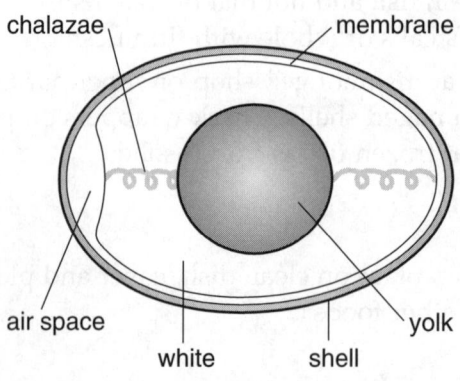

Shell: calcium carbonate, a thin membrane, an air space
White: jelly-like substance with water, proteins (albumin), vitamins
Yolk: mainly fat with protein held together by chalazae

NUTRITIVE VALUE

Proteins: rich source of HBV proteins
    White has many proteins e.g. albumin
    Yolk proteins e.g. livetin, vitellin
Carbohydrates: none in eggs
Lipids: mainly in the yolk, also cholesterol
Minerals: white has sulphur; yolk has calcium, iron, sulphur, phosphorus
Vitamins: fat-soluble A, D, E and K, also B group
Water: high water content, less in yolk than in white

DIETETIC VALUE

Eggs provide 100% high biological value proteins. Eggs are a good alternative to meat, poultry and fish. As eggs lack carbohydrates, serve with starchy foods. Because of their saturated fat and cholesterol content, eggs should be used with caution. Eggs provide iron but lack vitamin C to help absorption. Serve eggs with vitamin C-rich foods e.g. salads. Eggs are a versatile food in the diet. They are suitable for savoury and sweet dishes.

SHOPPING FOR EGGS

Buy from a clean, busy shop with a good turnover of customers. Choose eggs that are correctly labelled, clean, fresh, free from blemishes. Check best before date.

LABELLING EGGS

Information given on egg boxes includes:
- Country of origin
- Name of producer and registration number of packing station
- Product name and quantity
- Class A, B, C, with A being the best quality
- Grade of egg: sizes from 1 to 7
- Extra (freshest eggs)
- Week number (1–52 weeks) and expiry date

A quality symbol may also be on the egg box. Free-range eggs must have free-range stamped on the box.

STORING EGGS

Store eggs with the pointed end down in the refrigerator away from strong smelling foods. Do not wash the eggs as this removes the outer protective coating. Use eggs in rotation.

USING EGGS

- Remove from the refrigerator and bring to room temperature
- Cook at low temperatures to avoid curdling
- Bowls must be spotlessly clean, free of fat, when whisking egg whites
- If adding eggs to a hot mixture, to avoid curdling, cool and then add
- Wash hands after using eggs, before handling other foods

EFFECTS OF HEAT/COOKING ON EGGS

- Proteins coagulate (white at 60°C, yolk at 68°C)
- Albumin changes colour, becomes opaque and insoluble on heating
- Overcooking causes curdling and eggs become indigestible
- Little loss of nutrients except B group vitamins
- Egg whites toughen and yolks become crumbly

USES OF EGGS IN COOKING

Method	Example
Aerating	Cakes, desserts, meringues, sponges, soufflés
Binding	Burgers, icings, omelettes, potato cakes, rissoles
Coating	Batters, coatings for fried foods (sweet/savoury)
On their own	Boiled, fried, poached, scrambled
Emulsifying	Fat and eggs in cakes, mayonnaise, sauces
Enriching	Adding to the food value of all dishes e.g. quiche
Garnishing	Halved, sieved or sliced for salads/savoury dishes
Glazing	Pastry flans, pies, scones, tarts
Thickening	Custards, quiches, sauces, soups

DAIRY PRODUCTS

MILK

NUTRITIVE VALUE

Proteins: high biological proteins
Carbohydrates: milk sugar, called lactose
Lipids: present as an emulsion, stabilised by casein and lecithin
Minerals: calcium, phosphorus, a little magnesium, potassium, lacks iron
Vitamins: vitamins A, D, B group, amounts vary with seasons, lacks vitamin C
Water: high water content

DIETETIC VALUE

Human milk is the perfect food for new born babies. Breast feeding babies is recommended. Milk is important in the diet of pregnant and nursing mothers. The essential nutrients for growth are present in the form of high biological value proteins (caseinogen, lactalbumin, lactoglobulin), calcium, phosphorus and vitamins. Milk is an important source of vitamins A, D, riboflavin and other B group vitamins. Fat is present in an easily digested form. Milk and milk products may be fortified with extra nutrients. Low-fat milk is suitable for low cholesterol and slimming diets. Use milk with vitamin C-, iron- and carbohydrate-rich foods.

REASONS FOR PROCESSING MILK

- Destroys micro-organisms
- Increases keeping qualities
- Develops flavour

METHODS AND EFFECTS OF PROCESSING

Condensed Milk

- Similar to evaporated milk
- Milk is pasteurised, 15% sugar added, milk is evaporated to half its volume, homogenised, canned and sterilised. Used mainly for desserts
- Heat treatment is 115°C for 20 minutes

Effects of processing: loss of vitamins and water, very sweet taste

Dehydration

- Whole or skimmed milk may be dehydrated
- Milk is homogenised, evaporated, dried by spray drying or roller drying and packed

Effects of processing: water is removed, replaced when reconstituted, some loss of flavour and nutrients, sometimes fortified with vitamins

Evaporated Milk
- Milk is pasteurised, homogenised, evaporated to half its volume, homogenised, canned and sterilised
- Heat treatment is 115°C for 20 minutes

Effects of processing: some loss of vitamins and water, flavour changes, keeps indefinitely

Homogenisation
- Fat globules are reduced by forcing milk through small valves before pasteurisation or other methods of processing

Effects of processing: little loss of vitamins, flavour is altered, milk is creamy to taste, fat is distributed evenly

Pasteurisation
- Milk is pasteurised at 72°C for 15 seconds, cooled quickly to 10°C, packed, sealed

Effects of processing: bacteria is destroyed, loss of vitamin C and thiamine, changes in flavour, easily digested

Skimmed Milk
- Fat is removed along with the fat-soluble vitamins A and D

Effect of processing: flavour is altered

Sterilisation
- Milk is homogenised, bottled and sterilised at 110°C for 30 minutes

Effects of processing: loss of vitamins, flavour is altered, keeps for months, less digestible than other processed milk

Ultra-Heat Treatment
- Milk temperature is raised to 132°C for 1 second, cooled quickly to 10°C, sealed in lined cartons. Used in restaurants/catering industries

Effects of processing: loss of vitamins, flavour changes

Effects of Heat/Cooking on Milk
- Micro-organisms are destroyed
- Protein coagulates, a skin forms on the surface

- Flavour changes, becomes sweeter in condensed milk
- Loss of vitamin C and B group, varies with type
- Overheating causes curdling

MILK PRODUCTS

Milk products include butter, cheese, cream and yoghurt.

BUTTER

Butter is manufactured from cream. Fat globules are separated from the liquid in the cream. The liquid, buttermilk, is drained off, salt is added, butter is wrapped and packed for distribution. There are regulations as to the fat and water content of butter: 80% butter fat must be present.

Nutritive value
Proteins: small amounts of HBV protein
Carbohydrates: traces of milk sugar, lactose
Lipids: high percentage of concentrated saturated animal fats
Minerals: some calcium, phosphorus, added salt
Vitamins: fat-soluble vitamins A, D and E
Water: low water content

Types of Butter
Cream butter, dairy spreads, low-fat, spreadable, unsalted butter.

Culinary Uses
- Cake making e.g. Christmas cake
- Fillings for cakes e.g. sponges
- Potatoes e.g. creamed
- Sauces e.g. roux
- Sautéing meat, vegetables
- Spreads for sandwiches

CHEESE
Classification

Class	Examples
Hard	Cheddar, Cheshire, Gruyère, Parmesan, Wexford
Semi-hard	Caerphilly, Edam, Gouda, Irish Blue, Stilton
Soft	Brie, Camembert, Ricotta, Mozzarella

Other Types
Blue-veined: Irish Blue, Stilton
Irish Farmhouse: Abbeyleix Blue, Coolea, Derrynaflan
Unripened: Cottage (plain and flavoured), Ricotta

Composition
Cow's, goat's or sheep's milk are the main ingredient in cheese making. The composition of cheese varies depending on the source of the milk and its fat content.

Nutritive Value
Proteins: rich source of concentrated HBV protein
Carbohydrates: none present
Lipids: varies with cheese, high in cheddar, low in cottage cheese
Minerals: calcium, phosphorus, traces of sodium and iron
Vitamins: vitamins A, B group, some vitamin D
Water: varies with cheese

Dietetic Value
Cheese is a reasonably inexpensive concentrated source of protein and energy. It is a good alternative to meat, fish and poultry. Cheese is an excellent source of calcium and phosphorus. Cottage cheese is low in calcium. Cheese is particularly valuable in the diets of young children, teenagers, pregnant and nursing women. Some individuals find cheese difficult to digest. Cheese is generally high in saturated fats, except for cottage cheese. As it contains no carbohydrates, cheese should be served with carbohydrate-rich foods. Increase the mineral and vitamin content of a meal by serving fresh salads with cheese dishes. Cheese is suitable for snacks and packed lunches for children and adults.

Manufacturing Cheese
Milk is pasteurised. Lactic acid bacteria are added. The milk sours. Lactose changes to lactic acid. An enzyme, rennet, added to milk, coagulates protein producing curds (solids) and whey. The whey is drained off, curds are chopped, heated, pressed, salted and more whey is removed. Pressing removes excess whey as cheese is put into moulds to form hard or semi-hard cheeses. Flavours develop further during the ripening process in strictly controlled environments. The type of cheese determines the length of the ripening process.

Buying, Storing and Using Cheese
- Buy in small amounts
- Store in the refrigerator, wrapped in greaseproof paper
- Use quickly, check date stamps
- Bring cheese to room temperature to develop flavours

Culinary Uses
Grated as toppings/garnishes, in desserts, quiches, pizzas, pasta dishes, salads, sauces, as a snack, for cheeseboards and to increase value of foods.

Effect of Heat/Cooking on Cheese
- Protein coagulates and shrinks
- Fat melts
- Overcooking causes fat to separate and become stringy
- Dry heat causes cheese to brown
- Overcooked cheese is indigestible
- Little change in nutritive value

YOGHURT
Skimmed milk and whole milk are used to make yoghurt. Yoghurt is a fermented milk, thickened by a culture of lactic acid bacteria. It has a creamy consistency and slightly acid flavour. Nutritive value is determined by the type of milk used, fruits or fruit purée added.

Nutritive Value
Check nutritive value of milk. Carbohydrates are in the form of added sugar, fruits or fruit purée. Low-fat varieties are available.

Dietetic Value
Yoghurt is an excellent food in the diet of babies, children, teenagers, pregnant and nursing mothers and the elderly. It is convenient and easy to digest. It contains high biological value proteins and is a good source of calcium, which is essential for healthy bones and teeth. Low fat yoghurts are ideal for those on low fat diets. Yoghurts are ideal as a snack food.

Types of Yoghurt
Fruit, Greek, low-fat, milk-yoghurt drinks, natural, set yoghurts

Culinary Uses
As a snack, served as a topping on desserts, chopped fruits and breakfast cereals, in dips, milk shakes, sauces, soups, casseroles and curries, as an alternative to cream.

CEREALS

The sources of cereals are the grains of cultivated grasses e.g. barley, oats, maize, millet, rice, rye and wheat. Cereal products include biscuits, breakfast cereals, cakes, cornflakes, corn oil, a variety of flours (wheat, rye, rice), muesli, noodles, oatmeal, pasta, popcorn, rice (brown, ground, polished) and rice cakes.

STRUCTURE OF A WHEAT GRAIN

Cereals are composed of the outer husk, bran layer, aleurone layer, starchy endosperm and germ.

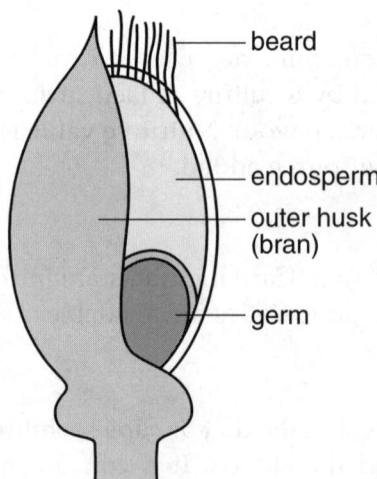

- The Endosperm contains the energy store of the grain, mainly of starch, the protein gluten and B group vitamins.
- The Husk contains cellulose, the husk is high in fibre or roughage, minerals (calcium, iron, phosphorus) and a rich supply of B group vitamins.
- The Germ contains protein, fat, vitamin E and B group and the nutrients for the germination of a new plant.

NUTRITIVE VALUE

Proteins: LBV proteins, main protein is gluten, deficient in some essential amino acids
Carbohydrates: high in starch, cellulose in outer husk
Lipids: traces in the germ
Minerals: calcium, iron, phosphorus
Vitamins: rich supply of B group vitamins, some vitamin E
Water: low water content: approximately 13%

DIETETIC VALUE

Cereals form the staple food of many countries and are an excellent source of energy. Protein present is of low biological value. Coeliacs are unable to absorb the gluten from wheat so they must avoid wheaten products. Unprocessed cereals provide roughage in the diet and B group vitamins. Processing removes the outer husks and vitamins, leaving behind high levels of starch. The absorption of calcium and iron is inhibited by the phytic acid also present in cereals. Nutrients are added during processing of some cereals. Serve cereals with vitamin-, mineral- and protein-rich foods.

DIETARY DISEASES ASSOCIATED WITH CEREALS

BERI-BERI
- Occurs in countries where polished rice is the staple food
- Results from a lack of B group vitamin, thiamine (removed during processing)

PELLAGRA
- Occurs in countries where maize, which lacks tryptophan, is the staple diet
- A lack of niacin results (the human body uses tryptophan to make niacin)

EFFECTS OF HEAT/COOKING ON CEREALS

- Proteins coagulate and set e.g. bread
- Cellulose softens and absorbs moisture
- Moist heat causes starch grains to burst and thicken liquids
- Dry heat causes starch grains to burst and absorb moisture
- Starch on outer surfaces changes to dextrin in dry heat
- Loss of some B group vitamins

MILLING OF WHEAT

Cleaning: washing, drying and conditioning of grains
Blending: a mixture of wheats are blended to create a 'grist'
Break rolling: metal rollers used to split open the grain (wholemeal flour)
Sieving: germ and bran are removed
Rolling and sieving: removes the germ and bran completely, produces white flour
Additives: bleaches and improvers are added, improves flour
Packing: flour is weighed and packed

FLOUR CHART

Types	Key points
Gluten-free flour	Protein gluten is removed, used to make products for coeliacs
Self-raising flour	A raising agent is added to white flour
Strong flour	High gluten content flour, used with yeast, for rich pastry
Wheatenmeal flour	Some germ, B group vitamins and bran removed, 85% extraction
Wheat germ	A mixture of cooked germ and white flour
Wholemeal flour	None of the grain is removed, 100% extraction
Stone ground flour	Two stones replace the metal rollers during milling, 100% extraction
White flour	Bran, germ removed with fat, less B group vitamins, the starchy endosperm remains, 75% extraction

Gluten: gluten is a protein found in wheat. When moistened gluten becomes elastic. The elastic properties of gluten allow dough to be stretched during the making of bread. Dough rises in the oven as gases expand. It then sets and forms a crust.

NUTRITIVE VALUE OF FLOUR

Proteins: LBV protein, higher in wholemeal than in white
Carbohydrates: high levels of starch in white flour, dietary fibre in wholemeal
Lipids: some present in wholemeal, none present in white flour
Minerals: calcium, iron and phosphorus
Vitamins: wholemeal provides B group vitamins, removed during the early stages in processing white flour
Water: low water content

OTHER CEREAL PRODUCTS

Pasta
- Good alternative to potatoes or rice
- Available in many shapes and colours, fresh or dried
- Is a nutritious healthy carbohydrate food
- Can be used in a variety of ways

Uses
Cold in salads, as a starter, a main dish, as part of the main course, instead of rice or potatoes or as an accompaniment to a buffet meal

Shapes
Cannelloni, lasagne, macaroni, noodles, ravioli, shells, spaghetti, spirals, stars, tagliatelle, tortellini and vermicelli

Types based on Colour
Brown wholemeal pasta, pasta tricolore with egg, spinach and tomato, pasta verde with spinach, red pasta with tomato and traditional white pasta

Rice
Types and Uses
Brown rice: outer husk removed. Contains more B group vitamins than other rices. Takes longer to cook. Uses: casseroles, curries and salads
White rice: germ and bran removed. Uses: savoury dishes
Easy cook rice: steam processed so that it cooks quickly. Uses: savoury dishes
Patna or long-grain rice: served with savoury dishes e.g. curry, sweet and sour, casseroles
Italian or medium-grain rice. Uses: risottos, salads
Carolina or short-grain rice. Uses: sweet dishes, milk pudding
Cook-in-bag rice: faster to cook and is convenient in emergencies. Uses: a variety of dishes.

Rice Products
Breakfast cereals, ground rice, rice cakes, rice flour, canned rice pudding, carton creamed rice

HOME BAKING: BREAD AND CAKES

RAISING AGENTS

Raising agents ensure that gas is produced in the dough. On heating, gas expands, the dough rises and sets. Gluten (protein in flour) becomes sticky when moistened enabling the dough to stretch until the crust sets. Gas may be produced because of a chemical reaction, a biological reaction or by the introduction of air.

Raising agents	Type	Examples
Air	Natural	Egg sponge
Baking powder	Chemical	Madeira cakes
Bread soda + sour milk	Chemical	Wholemeal bread
Yeast	Biological	Croissants, brack, breads

THE NATURAL REACTIONS
- Air is introduced by beating, creaming, folding, rolling, rubbing-in, sieving and whisking
- Steam is introduced during cooking in batters, cakes and choux pastry

THE CHEMICAL REACTION
Baking powder contains an acid and an alkali. Bread soda is the alkali and sour milk is the acid and the liquid.

Acid + Alkali + Liquid => Carbon Dioxide (CO_2) raises the dough

THE BIOLOGICAL REACTION
Yeast reacts with flour and sugar (foods) in the presence of moisture (eggs, milk, water) and warmth. This biological reaction in home baking is called fermentation.

Yeast + Food + Moisture + Warmth => Alcohol + CO_2 + energy

THE FERMENTATION PROCESS
During the fermentation process the enzymes present in flour and yeast react. The enzymes are diastase in flour, maltase, sucrase and zymase in yeast. The actions involved in fermentation are:

Enzyme/source	Acts on	Produces
Diastase (flour)	Starch (flour)	Maltose
Maltase (yeast)	Maltose (flour)	Glucose
Sucrase (yeast)	Sucrose (sugar)	Glucose + Fructose
Zymase (yeast)	Glucose and Fructose	CO_2 and Alcohol

Carbon dioxide gas raises the dough and the alcohol evaporates during baking.

TYPES OF YEAST

The three types of yeast are dried yeast, fast action yeast and fresh yeast. Fresh yeast should be moist, grey-putty in colour and have a pleasant smell.

GUIDELINES FOR BAKING WITH YEAST

- Choose top quality fresh yeast, check 'best before' label on dried yeast
- Choose strong flour with high gluten content
- Weigh ingredients accurately, proportions must be correct
- Ensure kitchen, ingredients and utensils are warm
- Blend fresh yeast in a little warmed liquid, add dry yeast to dry ingredients
- Kneading dough activates and develops the gluten
- Place dough in a greased bowl, cover with damp cloth
- Rise slowly in a warm place (proving)
- Once it has risen knock back, knead again
- Shape dough, place in tins, prove again (second proving)
- Bake in a hot oven to prevent yeast from rising further

TOO MUCH

- Fat inhibits the action of yeast
- Heat kills the yeast
- Sugar prevents fermentation

CHORLEY WOOD PROCESS

Using small amounts of vitamin C speeds up the fermentation of yeast in yeast bread making. Rising time is reduced by one third. The use of vitamin C is referred to as the Chorley Wood Process.

CLASSIFICATION OF CAKES

Class	Underlying principle	Examples
All-in-one	Mix all ingredients together	Madeira, sponges
Creaming	Cream fat into sugar	Fruit cake, Madeira
Melted fat	Melt fat, etc., add to dry ingredients	Gingerbread, boiled fruit cake
Rubbing-in	Rub fat into flour	Scones, small cakes, yeast breads
Whisking	Whisk eggs and sugar together	Flan cases, meringues, swiss roll

PASTRY

CLASSIFICATION

Types	Variations	Example(s) of use
Shortcrust	Plain	Flans, pies, tarts
	Rich	Mince pies
	Cheese	Cheese biscuits, cheese straws, quiches
	Sweet	Fruit flans
Rich or Flaked	Flaky pastry	Mince pies, sausage rolls, tarts
	Rough puff	Mince pies, sausage rolls
	Puff pastry	Vol-au-vents, pies (savoury/sweet)
Hot	Choux pastry	Eclairs, profiteroles
	Hot water crust	Savoury pies
Suet		Steamed puddings
Filo		Spring rolls
		Fruit in filo for dessert

GUIDELINES FOR MAKING PASTRY

- Ensure kitchen, ingredients and utensils are cold
- Weigh ingredients accurately

- Enclose as much air by sieving, mixing, folding, etc.
- Handle pastry as little as possible, hands may be warm
- Mix with a cold knife, add water carefully
- When rolling do not stretch pastry
- Refrigerate to relax pastry before use
- Bake in a hot oven so that starch cells burst and absorb the fat

FRUIT

Fruit is a versatile food available all year round in a variety of forms. Fruits are available canned, bottled, fresh, frozen and also as part of other products.

CLASSIFICATION CHART

Berries	Blackberries, blackcurrants, gooseberries, raspberries, strawberries
Citrus	Grapefruits, lemons, limes, oranges, satsumas
Dried	Currants, dates, figs, raisins, sultanas
Hard	Apples, pears
Stone	Apricots, cherries, nectarines, peaches, plums
Miscellaneous	Bananas, melons, pineapples, rhubarb

NUTRITIVE VALUE OF FRESH FRUIT

Proteins: traces present, dried fruit best source
Carbohydrates: cellulose, pectin, starches, sugars
Lipids: none in most fruits, except avocados, bananas and olives
Minerals: calcium, iron and traces of other minerals
Vitamins: good supply of vitamin C, some B group and A
Water: very high in fresh fruit, lower in dried fruit

DIETETIC VALUE

Fresh fruits are valuable in the diet because of their vitamin C content. Fruit is an excellent source of dietary fibre, which acts as roughage in the diet. Fruits may be used raw or cooked, in savoury or sweet dishes. The high water content makes fruit a refreshing food to use as a snack in between meals, as starter or dessert and in packed lunches. Fruit should be included in every diet. The vitamins and minerals present protect the body against disease. Vitamin C assists in the absorption of iron.

BUYING FRUIT

- Buy fruits in season when they are cheapest
- Choose top quality fruits, check the grade
- Choose just ripe fruits, loose rather than packed
- Use as soon as possible, buy in small quantities

EFFECTS OF PREPARING AND COOKING FRUIT

- Oxidation occurs during preparation of apples and pears
- Enzymes and micro-organisms are destroyed
- Texture softens, colours and flavour change
- Fruit becomes more digestible, cellulose breaks down
- Vitamin C is destroyed
- Vitamins and minerals leech into cooking liquid
- Overcooking causes fruit to break up
- Some metals react with fruit i.e. nutritive value and colour changes

EFFECTS OF PROCESSING ON FRUIT

Canning: causes texture to soften, reduces vitamin C, increases sugar (syrup)
Drying: reduces vitamins A, B group and C
Freezing: causes little nutritional changes but texture changes

CULINARY USES OF FRUITS

As garnishes, decorations, starters, snacks, beverages, in milk shakes, salads, sauces, main courses, desserts, with cheeseboard and preserves.

VEGETABLES

CLASSIFICATION CHART

Class	Examples
Bulbs	Garlic, onion, shallot
Greens	Cabbage, kale, lettuce, spinach, sprouts
Flowers	Broccoli, cauliflower
Fruits	Aubergine, courgette, cucumber, marrow, pepper, pumpkin, tomato
Fungi	Mushroom
Roots & Tubers	Carrot, parsnip, potato, radish, turnip
Pulses	Beans, lentils, peas

NUTRITIVE VALUE

Proteins: pulses provide the best supply of protein, very low in most vegetables
Carbohydrates: cellulose in skins of all vegetables, starch in potatoes and pulse vegetables, a little sugar in beetroot, carrots, onions and tomatoes
Lipids: most deficient, except a little in olives and soya beans
Minerals: calcium, iron, phosphorus and sulphur
Vitamins: excellent supply of carotene, vitamins A, B group, C
Water: high water content, varying from 75 to 95% in fresh vegetables

DIETETIC VALUE

Vegetables are essential in all diets because of their rich supply of carbohydrates, minerals and vitamins. Cellulose in vegetables is an important source of dietary fibre which adds bulk to the diet. Vegetables contain anti-oxidant vitamins A, C and a little E. Vegetables are an important source of minerals. Green vegetables are an excellent source of calcium and iron. Phosphorus and sulphur are also supplied by vegetables. Pulses are important in the diet of vegetarians because of their proteins. Vegetables are a refreshing and versatile food in the diet. Vegetables lack vitamin D and B12, so serve with foods rich in these nutrients.

BUYING VEGETABLES

- Buy when in season as they are cheapest
- Choose clean, fresh, medium-sized vegetables, even in colour, without blemishes
- Choose crisp fresh greens, roots and tubers that appear heavy for their size
- Check grade, 'best before' label and buy in small quantities
- Buy loose vegetables if possible

STORING VEGETABLES

Remove vegetables from plastic wrapping at home. Store salads and greens in the vegetable drawer at the bottom of the refrigerator. Choose a cool, dry, dark, well-ventilated place for roots and tubers. On returning from shopping put frozen vegetables into the freezer immediately to prevent them thawing out. Store pulse vegetables in air-tight jars. Use fresh vegetables as soon as possible. The quality of fresh vegetables deteriorates rapidly.

PREPARING VEGETABLES

- Use raw whenever possible
- Wash or scrub and peel as appropriate
- Avoid early preparation and steeping
- Prepare according to kind, just before the meal
- Using a sharp knife to prevent vitamin loss, trim sparingly
- Wash under running water to remove all traces of insects and soil

COOKING VEGETABLES

Cook vegetables in a small amount of water, for the shortest possible cooking time, in a saucepan with a tightly fitting lid, to retain the vitamins and minerals.

Effects of Cooking on Vegetables

- Enzymes and micro-organisms are destroyed
- Cellulose is softened, starch cells burst, vegetables become more digestible
- Colour, flavour and texture change
- A great amount of vitamin C is lost
- Minerals and vitamins leech into the cooking liquid
- Overcooking causes vegetables to break up and become soggy

PROCESSING VEGETABLES

Bottling, canning, dehydration, freezing and pickling

Effects of Processing on Vegetables

Canning: vegetables soften, texture is changed, vitamin C destroyed, loss of B group vitamins

Dehydration: colour, flavour and texture change, vitamin C destroyed, loss of B group vitamins

Freezing: nutritive value remains almost unchanged, fruit vegetables loose their shape and texture changes. Most vegetables freeze well, some loss of vitamin C during freeze-drying

GRADING OF FRUIT AND VEGETABLES

Class Extra	Top Quality
Class 1	Good Quality
Class 2	Some blemishes, defects in colour and shape
Class 3	Inferior quality but marketable

FATS AND OILS

CLASSIFICATION

Fats may be classified as saturated or unsaturated.

Saturated or Animal Fats

Characteristics: solid at room temperature, generally saturated
Sources: butter, eggs, fish, meat, meat fats (lard, suet), milk

Unsaturated or Vegetable Fats

Characteristics: liquid at room temperature, generally unsaturated
Sources: cooking fats, margarine, oils (nuts, seeds)

CULINARY USES OF FATS AND OILS

- Creaming, flavouring, frying, shortening, spreading
- As emulsifying agents in a variety of sweet and savoury dishes
- As anti-staling agents, help keep bread and cakes fresher for longer
- As emulsions in mayonnaise, salad dressings and sauces

- For sautéing, frying and other cooking methods
- For greasing baking tins

COOKING FATS

These are manufactured mainly from vegetable oils and are suitable for cooking at high temperatures. Cooking fats lack flavour. Uses: frying, pastry, cakes.

VEGETABLE OILS

Sources: maize, nuts, olives, palm, rape seed and soya bean
Uses: frying, brushing food for cooking, dressings, salads.

SUMMARY OF THE MANUFACTURE OF VEGETABLE OILS

- Cleaning, crushing, heating and pressing of plants
- Removing impurities
- Adding antioxidants, anti-spattering agents, colours and flavours
- Blending of oils

MARGARINE

Margarine is manufactured from vegetable oils by:
- Extracting and refining oils from vegetable sources
- Adding hydrogen gas, in the presence of a catalyst, to harden the mixture
- Adding and blending colourings, emulsifiers, flavourings, nutrients, other oils, salt and skimmed milk
- Churning these ingredients to regulate consistency using a rotator machine
- Lowering the temperature, kneading, moulding, shaping, weighing, wrapping and packing

TYPES OF MARGARINE/SPREADS

All purpose, low-fat spread, luxury, polyunsaturated spreads.

PLANNING, PREPARING AND PRESENTING MEALS

When organising meals for the family plan a weekly menu and shop ahead. Use a shopping list to avoid waste and impulse buying. Check that the menu is nutritionally balanced and allows time for adequate preparation, cooking and serving.

Select foods in season when they are at their cheapest. Choose a variety of cooking methods, suiting the food and time available. Plan for garnishes and accompaniments.

GUIDELINES FOR PLANNING MEALS

WHEN PLANNING MEALS CONSIDER

- Type of meal e.g. breakfast, lunch, dinner, special occasion
- Nutritional requirements of individuals based on age, lifestyle, occupation (sedentary, manual)
- Special dietary needs e.g. coeliac, gluten-free, high-fibre, low-fat, vegetarian
- Individual preferences, if appropriate and practical
- Time available, choose fast methods of cooking, serve salads
- Time of year, serve light chilled foods in summer, piping hot dishes in winter.
- Variety of fresh foods available, allow variety in planning, cooking and presentation
- Number of people
- Money available, budgetary restrictions, luxury foods
- Equipment available and cooking skills needed for each dish
- Colours, flavours and textures
- Presentation and garnishes/decorations

POINTS TO CONSIDER WHEN PREPARING MEALS

- Rules of personal, food and kitchen hygiene
- Guidelines for safe preparation of individual foods e.g. eggs, chicken
- Lifestyle and time available for preparation
- Use of herbs, spices and garnished to introduce variety

POINTS TO CONSIDER WHEN PRESENTING MEALS

- Set table using sparkling clean cutlery, dishes, glasses and table linen
- Put heat-resistant mats on table

- Arrange filled condiment sets in groups on table
- Use plain dishes for savoury foods, decorated dishes for sweet foods
- Hot food should be served piping hot on heated plates
- Serve cold foods chilled on cold plates
- Arrange food neatly on plates wiping spills off edges using damp kitchen paper
- Place meats towards centre with sauces around edge of meat
- Serve sauces, vegetables and other accompaniments separately in suitable dishes
- Select garnishes and decorations to compliment colour, flavour and texture
- Avoid keeping foods warm, serve immediately when cooked

DECORATIONS AND GARNISHES

DECORATIONS
Almonds (flakes), cherries (halves, whole), chocolate (grated, leaves, melted), cream (piped)

GARNISHES
Chives (chopped), croutons, cucumber (slices, twists) lemon, lime or orange (slices, twists), mint (chopped, sprigs), parsley (finely chopped, sprigs), radishes, yoghurt or cream

SHOPPING AND COOKING ON A BUDGET

WHEN COOKING ON A RESTRICTED BUDGET
- Check food cupboards, refrigerator and freezer
- Plan the menu for the week and make a shopping list
- Shop once a week or month to save time and transport
- Buy the best quality foods that you can afford
- Know the food prices in various shops and supermarkets
- Check out own brand products for quality and price
- Check if buying a product in bulk is less expensive
- Buy perishable goods daily e.g. milk
- Choose vegetables in season, cheaper than out of season
- Select cheaper cuts of meat, they are just as nutritious as expensive cuts
- Examine all food labels, check best before date
- Buy convenience foods for emergency use only
- If available make maximum use of a freezer

COOKERY AND FUEL ECONOMY

- Serve foods raw where possible e.g. salads, fruits
- Make full use of oven, cooking a full meal in it rather than one item
- Have a baking morning or day, freeze the extra items
- Cook double quantities, have the extra next day or freeze for use later
- Make use of rising oven heat to complete casseroles
- Use steamers and pressure cookers on the hob to economise on fuel
- Make jams and preserves in large quantities
- If replacing a cooker, choose one with new economy features

EFFICIENT WORKING METHODS

- Plan ahead, make lists and stick to them
- Organise everything in a logical sequence
- Plan menus with budget, time, effort and energy in mind
- Make maximum use of labour saving devices
- Weigh ingredients, organise equipment before you start cooking
- Wash up equipment used as you go along, keep all surfaces clean and tidy

EFFICIENT TIME MANAGEMENT

- Plan menus on a weekly basis
- Consider the time available
- Work out time plans
- Plan menus to include cold dishes that need no cooking
- Choose meals that can be cooked in oven, on hob, in a steamer or pressure cooker
- Avoid individual dishes that require to be cooked on their own in the oven
- As the food is cooking, set the table and organise the serving dishes

GUIDELINES FOR ENTERTAINING AT HOME

ADVANCE PLANNING AND ORGANISATION

- Invite guests well in time, do not leave it to the last minute
- Plan and prepare as much as possible in advance
- Design the menu to suit the occasion and the guests
- Make a shopping list and shop early
- Choose dishes that suit your culinary skills
- Do not test new dishes on guests

- Avoid highly spiced dishes e.g. curries
- Buy perishables on the day
- Set table evening before, organise extra chairs and tables if required

Preparation on the Day
- Remove prepared dishes from the freezer
- Check table, ventilate room, organise flowers for table and side tables
- Collect ingredients, equipment and serving dishes
- Prepare foods for cooking, cover and put in fridge until required
- Cook dishes that cannot be cooked in advance just before serving
- Wash dirty utensils and put away

Presentation and Serving
- Place heat-resistant mats on the table
- Serve all dishes as soon as they are cooked
- Wipe spills from edges and garnish or decorate
- Serve at once: hot dishes piping hot, cold dishes cold/chilled

Buffet Parties
- Cook and freeze some dishes in advance of the day
- Provide a variety of colours, flavours and textures
- Choose dishes that are easy to serve
- Choose foods that are in bite size pieces, manageable with a fork
- Serve non-alcoholic drinks and wines from a separate table
- Arrange cutlery, glasses, plates, serviettes and serving spoons so that they are easy to reach
- Arrange condiment sets and serving cutlery
- Use heat-resistant mats under hot dishes
- Place hot dishes on the table just as guests are ready to eat
- Keep chilled foods covered until required, place on table at the last minute
- Place chairs around the room

Allocate the task of pouring drinks, gathering dirty plates, dishes and cutlery to someone else so that you can enjoy entertaining family and friends

6

MICROBIOLOGY

Microbiology is the study of micro-organisms i.e. bacteria, fungi (moulds, yeasts) and viruses.

CONDITIONS ENCOURAGING GROWTH OF MICRO-ORGANISMS

- Food
- Light/darkness
- Moisture
- Oxygen
- Specific pH levels
- Warmth

FOOD

Micro-organisms get their food from other sources. As they do not contain chlorophyll they are unable to produce their own food. An enzyme is released by the micro-organisms onto a ready made food supply. This breaks down the food into simpler substances, which can then be absorbed through their cell walls. Micro-organisms can be parasites or saprophytes.

- Parasites survive on living matter
- Saprophytes live on dead or decaying matter

LIGHT/DARKNESS

Most grow best without light and are destroyed by strong ultra-violet sunlight.

MOISTURE

Water is essential for micro-organisms to live. Food sources provide the water for metabolic processes. Micro-organisms cannot use ice. Some produce spores in the absence of water.

OXYGEN

Micro-organisms have different requirements in relation to oxygen e.g. some require oxygen, some do not require oxygen, others can function with or without oxygen. Micro-organisms may be grouped according to their oxygen requirements.

Group	Oxygen requirements
Aerobic	Need oxygen to survive
Anaerobic	Do not need oxygen
Facultative	Can function with or without oxygen

SPECIFIC PH LEVELS

Most micro-organisms prefer a neutral pH level i.e. pH 7. They are destroyed by strong acids or alkalis. Some micro-organisms prefer slightly acidic or alkaline environments, just either side of pH 7.

WARMTH

Micro-organisms can be grouped according to their reaction to temperatures.

Group	Temperature requirements
Mesophiles	+30 to +45°C (most micro-organisms in this group)
Psychrophiles	−5 to +20°C (low temperatures)
Thermophiles	+55 to +75°C (high temperatures)

Temperatures	What happens to micro-organisms
−5 to −25°C	Growth inhibited, micro-organisms inactivated
+30 to +45°C	Optimum temperature for growth, micro-organisms flourish
70°C+	Most micro-organisms are destroyed, except some bacteria
100°C+	All bacteria destroyed except heat-resistant spores
121°C	Heat-resistant spores destroyed by maintaining temperature for 15 minutes

DESTROYING MICRO-ORGANISMS

The spread of micro-organisms can be controlled by:
- Cleaning agents e.g. disinfectant
- Removing moisture and ready made food supplies
- Increasing temperatures to high temperatures

- Strong acids and alkalis
- Using antibiotics
- Producing their own toxins and wastes
- Overcrowding of micro-organisms

BACTERIA

Bacteria are single-celled micro-organisms. Numbers double every 20 minutes. Bacteria can be parasites or saprophytes. Bacteria like other micro-organisms are also grouped according to their oxygen requirements: aerobic, anaerobic or facultative.

SOURCES OF BACTERIA

Air, animals, foods, plants, soil and water.

CLASSIFICATION OF BACTERIA ACCORDING TO SHAPE

- Bacillus (rods)
  Bacilli e.g. TB and Clostridia *(Clostridium botulinum, Escherichia coli, Salmonella)*

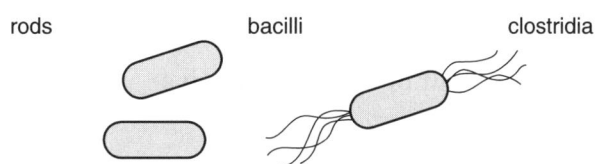

- Cocci (spheres)
  Coccus (singly), diplococci (pairs), staphylococci (clusters) or streptococci (chains)

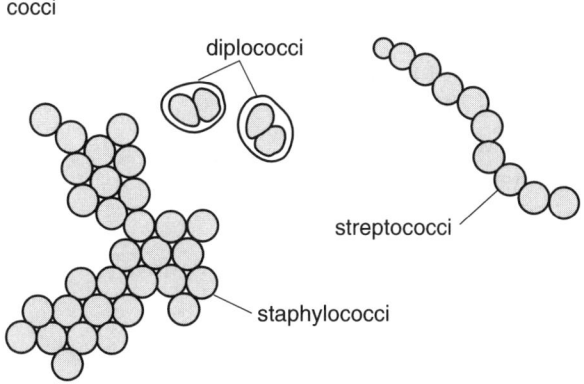

- Commas, Spirals or Twisted (variety of shapes) Spirilla e.g. Syphilis; and Vibrio e.g. Cholera

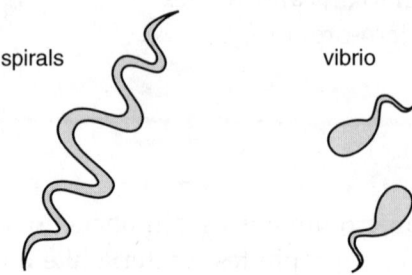

CLASSIFICATION OF BACTERIA ACCORDING TO GRAM STAIN

The steps involved in Gram staining bacteria are:
- Smear an agar filled plate with a culture
- Incubate in a suitable place
- Pour crystal violet dye over the sample to locate the bacteria
- Using distilled water, wash off the dye
- Pour solution of iodine over the culture to fix colour
- Add acetone to remove colour

Gram Staining Results Chart
Gram-Positive Bacteria
- Blue-black, the colour of crystal violet dye
- Thick single cell wall
- 2% lipid in cell wall
- Generally aerobic
- Non-mobile
- Spore producing
- Little resistance to antibiotics

Gram-Negative Bacteria
- Reddish, the colour of iodine
- Two thin layers in cell wall
- 20% lipid in cell wall
- Aerobic and anaerobic
- Mobile: have flagella
- Do not produce spores
- More resistant to antibiotics

STRUCTURE OF BACTERIAL CELL

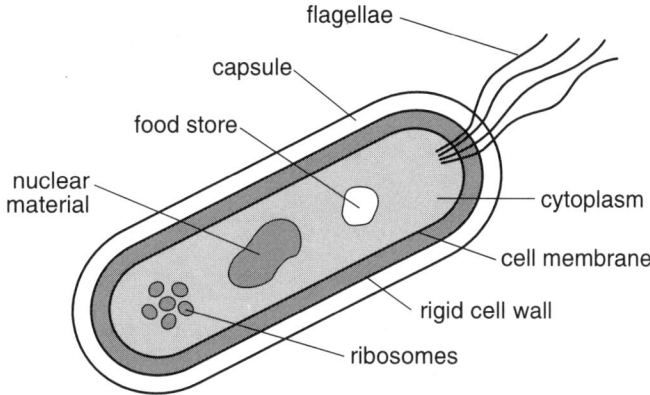

A bacterial cell consists of an outer, rigid cell wall, cell membrane and cytoplasm with nuclear material and ribosomes. Some bacterial cells have flagella to help them move and a capsule for protection.

Endospores: these are tough dormant cells produced by bacilli and clostridia when conditions are unsuitable for reproduction. Such spores are resistant to cold, heat and some chemicals. Endospores can be destroyed by dry heat (150°C for 1 hour) or steam (121°C for 15 minutes).

BENEFICIAL EFFECTS OF BACTERIA

- Important in treatment of waste
- Intestinal bacteria manufacture vitamins B and K
- Food production e.g. cheese, vinegar, yoghurt

DISADVANTAGES OF BACTERIA

- Spoilage of food
- Toxic food poisoning
- Infective food poisoning

DISEASES ASSOCIATED WITH BACTERIA

Boils, cholera, diphtheria, dysentery, food poisoning, meningitis, pneumonia, tetanus, typhoid

FUNGI

Like bacteria, fungi cannot manufacture their own food and are dependent on ready made sources to survive. Fungi can be parasites or saprophytes.

CLASSIFICATION

Moulds; Yeasts; Large fungi

BENEFITS OF FUNGI

Fungi are used in cooking (as ingredients), food production (cheese making, bread, vinegar, wine making), luxury foods and pharmaceutical industry.

MOULDS
Basic Structure

Spores are released from fungi to produce new fungi. When a single cell or spore lands on a ready made food source, it develops filaments or hyphae that grow into the food. Hyphae absorb nutrients and moisture from the food. A network of filaments, called a mycelium, develops.

Reproduction of Moulds

Asexual Reproduction

Hyphae grow vertically out of the mycelium and a spore-forming head emerges at the top called the sporangium (round) or conidia (branched). When mature, the sporangium or conidia release the spores, to be spread by water or air, to a medium where they reproduce.

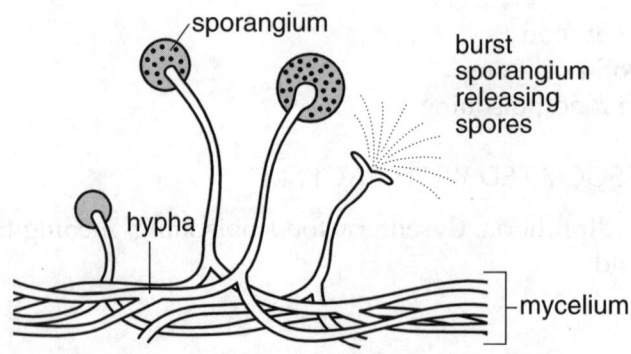

Sexual Reproduction

Sexual reproduction occurs when two hyphae from different fungi come into contact with each other and fuse together forming a zygospore. Spores form within the zygospore and under suitable conditions are released for germination.

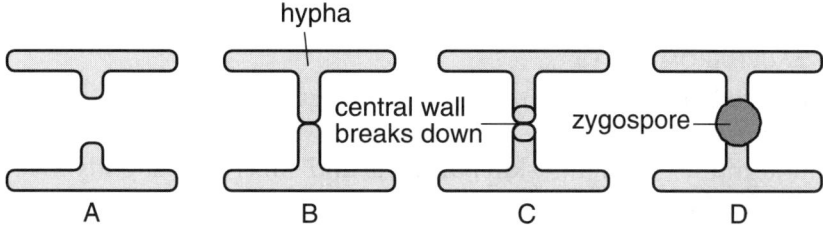

Mould Chart

Mould	Category	Colour	Reproduction	Shape	Sources
Aspergillus	Saprophyte	Blue-green	Asexual/sexual	Produce sporangia	Cereals, fruit
Mucor	Saprophyte	Fluffy white	Asexual/sexual	Produce sporangia	Bread, cakes
Rhizopus	Saprophyte	Black	Asexual	Produce sporangia	Bread, cakes, fruit, vegetables
Penicillium	Saprophyte	Greenish	Asexual	Produce conidia	Oranges, cheese, vegetables

BASIDIOMYCETES: LARGE FUNGI

Some large fungi are edible, others are poisonous. The extremely poisonous fungi can be fatal if eaten. Do not eat any wild mushroom that cannot be identified.

Examples of Edible Fungi: Mushrooms

More varieties of mushrooms have become available in the last few years. Examples include: commercially produced button mushroom, chanterelles, oyster mushrooms, morels and wild truffles.

Development of a Mushroom
- Mushroom spore develops a network of hyphae, forms a mycelium
- A stalk develops and pushes out of the ground with a cap
- Cap swells, bursts open and gills are visible underneath
- Gills darken, spores are released from between gills onto the ground and into the air

YEASTS: SACCHAROMYCETES
- Single-celled facultative, saprophytic fungi, destroyed by high temperatures
- Found in the air, on the skins of fruits and survive in slightly sweet and acidic foods
- Important source of B group vitamins, used in health products and food supplements
- Used in bread making, wine making and brewing

Structure
Yeasts have a thin single outer cell wall, cytoplasm filled with a nucleus, vacuoles and storage granules.

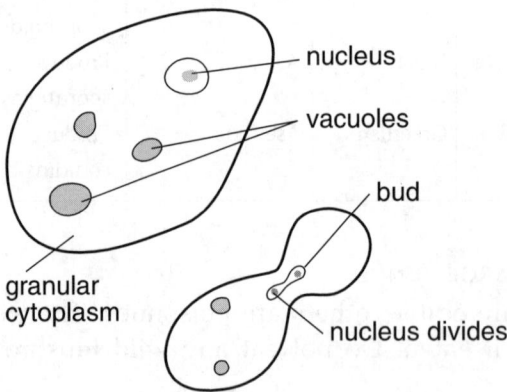

Reproduction of Yeast
- Reproduces asexually by the process called *budding*
- Requires a suitable medium, moisture, acid environment and warmth
- Small swelling forms and develops on the side of a single cell
- Cell nucleus divides, a wall forms, dividing the two cells
- New cell eventually separates from the main or parent cell
- New cell begins to bud or reproduce into chains of yeast cells

FOOD SPOILAGE AND CONTAMINATION

Causes	Examples
Animals and insects	Flies, mice, rats, pets (cats, dogs)
Chemicals	Antibiotics, insecticides, metals, pesticides
Clothing	Dirty aprons in kitchens
Enzymes	Present on food, in air
Micro-organisms	Moulds, yeasts, bacteria

TYPES OF FOOD SPOILAGE

Colour changes, fermentation, mould, rot, putrefaction and slime

SYMPTOMS OF FOOD POISONING

Symptoms include abdominal cramps, diarrhoea, fever, nausea, vomiting. Some or all of the symptoms may be present depending on the type of food poisoning.

HIGH RISK FOODS

Dairy products: cream, custards, eggs
Protein foods: fish including shellfish, meat, poultry
Reheated dishes: chicken, meats, pies, stews

CAUSES OF FOOD POISONING

BACTERIA

Infectious: eating food contaminated by pathogens
    Examples: *Salmonella, E. coli, Clostridia welchii*
Toxic: eating food containing toxins produced by bacteria outside the body
    Examples: *Staphylococci, Clostridia botulinum*

CHEMICALS

- Eating foods contaminated by poisonous chemicals
  Examples: additives, metals, insecticides, pesticides

NATURAL

- Eating poisonous fungi and plants
  Examples: some mushrooms, berries, plant leaves

FOOD POISONING BACTERIA

CLOSTRIDIUM BOTULINUM
- Toxic food poisoning bacteria
- One of the most serious forms of food poisoning, produces a deadly toxin that causes botulism, recovery can take months
- Rod-shaped, anaerobic, Gram-positive, produces spores and toxin
- Origins are decaying matter and soil, toxin produced in incorrectly canned foods e.g. fish
- Some symptoms include blurred vision, diarrhoea, dizziness, slurred speech, paralysis, death
- Destroyed by temperatures of 121°C if maintained for 5 minutes

CLOSTRIDIA PERFRINGENS (WELCHII)
- Infectious and toxic food poisoning bacteria
- Rod-shaped, anaerobic, Gram-positive, produces heat-resistant spores, toxin produced after eating contaminated food
- Spores live in air, dust, soil and water
- Sources include soil, intestines of animals and humans, contaminated meat/meat products
- Symptoms are abdominal pain, diarrhoea, sometimes nausea and vomiting

LISTERIA
- Infectious food poisoning bacteria causing listeriosis, can be fatal
- Rod-shaped, facultative, Gram-positive, no spores, psychrophilic, likes an acid pH
- Sources are contaminated animals and animal products (unpasteurised soft cheese, poultry) cook/chill products, raw vegetables
- Survives in soil and intestinal tracts
- Symptoms include fever, is serious for infants, pregnant women, elderly people

SALMONELLA
- Rod-shaped, mobile, facultative, Gram-negative, no spores
- Survives in human and animal intestines (farm animals, flies, pets, vermin)
- Sources include contaminated eggs, raw foods, sausages, shellfish, untreated water
- Symptoms include abdominal pain, diarrhoea, fever, nausea and vomiting

Staphylococci
- Round, mobile, facultative, Gram-positive, reproduce every 20 minutes
- Sources are human nose, saliva, throat, skin, passed on by unwashed hands to food
- Bacteria secrete an enzyme onto food to access nutrients
- Produce a toxin
- Symptoms include cramps, diarrhoea and nausea, short incubation period

PREVENTING FOOD CONTAMINATION

In Our Homes
- Clean and disinfect bathrooms, kitchens and lavatories daily
- Follow guidelines for personal, food and kitchen hygiene

Personal Hygiene
- Do not work with food if suffering from food poisoning
- Wash hands after handling cats, dogs and pets
- Wash hands after working in the garden
- Wash hands immediately after using the toilet
- Always wash hands before handling or cooking food
- Cover all cuts and abrasions with waterproof dressings
- Keep nails clean and short, tie up or cover hair
- Wear a clean apron
- Do not cough, sneeze or spit over food

Kitchen Hygiene
- Keep kitchen ventilated, open windows daily
- Keep all pets out of the kitchen
- Wash and disinfect all kitchen surfaces
- Wipe up spills as soon as they occur
- Disinfect drains and sinks regularly
- Clean out kitchen cupboards frequently
- Wash kitchen cloths, tea towels and hand towels daily
- Clean cooker, fridge and microwave oven regularly
- Empty, disinfect and wash kitchen bin regularly
- Sweep, wash and disinfect kitchen floor daily

FOOD HYGIENE
- Store all foods in appropriate places
- Handle all food as little as possible to prevent cross-contamination
- Have separate chopping boards for preparing raw and cooked foods
- Wash hands after preparing raw foods and always before handling cooked foods
- Store raw and cooked foods separately and covered
- Cook all foods correctly and thoroughly
- Store leftover cooked foods in the fridge
- Reheat leftover foods thoroughly to destroy bacteria
- Store frozen foods at the correct temperatures in the freezer
- Do not refreeze frozen foods, thaw food correctly
- Place cooked foods on shelves above uncooked foods in the fridge
- Use all foods by best before date

IMPLEMENTING LEGISLATION

Government safety rules and regulations help reduce the incidence of food poisoning. The implementation of these safety standards is carried out by:
- Inspecting farms, food manufacturing plants, catering, hotel and restaurant businesses, shops, markets and other suppliers of food
- Providing education for those involved in the production and preparation of foods whether in catering, hotel or restaurants or in the home

OTHER METHODS OF PREVENTION INCLUDE:
- Effective sewage treatment
- Pasteurisation and sterilisation of dairy products
- Preservation (home and commercial)
- Safe water systems (rural, community schemes)
- Sewage treatment plants
- Use of disinfectants and other chemicals

OTHER GOVERNMENT INITIATIVES

FOOD SAFETY AUTHORITY OF IRELAND

The Food Safety Authority of Ireland is an independent statutory body set up by the government. Its main aim is to reassure consumers on safety of food in Ireland and on Irish food aborad. It provides information and is operating on an interim basis. The Food Safety Authority has no enforcement powers at present. A Food Safety Information Centre has been set up by the Food Safety Authority.

MAKING A COMPLAINT ABOUT FOOD

Consumers with complaints regarding food or a food premises should contact the Environmental Health Officer in the local Health Board. The Public Health Doctor in the local Health Board deals with complaints about illness. Both services are confidential and consumer advice is provided on the appropriate course of action.

7

FOOD PRESERVATION

REASONS FOR PRESERVING FOODS

- Maintains natural colours, flavours, textures and nutritive value
- Avoids waste by preserving garden produce
- Saves money by availing of foods in season when they are cheapest
- Provides food in emergencies
- Provides food in a convenient, easy to store form
- Adds variety to the menu throughout the year
- Provides produce when out of season

PRINCIPLES OF FOOD PRESERVATION

- To destroy micro-organisms
- To prevent their re-entry into food
- To inhibit the activity of the enzymes present
- To maintain natural colours, flavours and textures

PRESERVATION PRINCIPALS IN ACTION

To flourish, enzymes and micro-organisms need:
    Warmth; Food; Moisture; Oxygen

By removing these conditions and processing foods, enzymes can be inactivated and micro-organisms destroyed.

Methods of preservation	Examples
Chemical treatments	Pickles, chutneys, ketchup, smoking
Bottling and canning	Fruits, vegetable, fish, meat products
Drying (removing moisture)	Dried foods e.g. soups, cake mixes
Freezing (removing warmth)	Frozen foods (fruits, vegetables)
Heat treatments	Jams, jellies, bottled fruits
Irradiation	Fruits, vegetables

HOME PRESERVATION

CHEMICAL PRESERVATION

Underlying Principle

The chemical is in a concentrated form. It draws moisture from the bacteria through the cell walls. The process of osmosis destroys any bacteria present.

Chemicals used	Some examples
Alcohol	Christmas mincemeat, conserves
Salt	Salted fish, meat, pickles, vegetables
Smoking (wood)	Fish, meat, poultry
Sugar	Jams, jellies, conserves
Vinegar	Chutneys, rollmop herrings

CHUTNEYS AND PICKLES

UNDERLYING PRINCIPLES

Chutneys are cooked to 100°C with vinegar, sugar, spices and salt. This destroys the micro-organisms and enzymes. Vinegar produces an acid pH level which is not favoured by the micro-organisms. Concentrations of salt, sugar and vinegar kill bacterial cells by osmosis.

Pickles are preserved in vinegar with salt, spices and sugar added. The high temperatures, vinegar, salt spices and sugar destroy the enzymes and bacteria.

Chutneys and pickles are sealed in jars to prevent the re-entry of micro-organisms. Chutneys and pickles can be served with cheese, cold meats, salads and hot dishes e.g. curries.

BOTTLING

UNDERLYING PRINCIPLE

Bottling is the process of preserving fruit by sterilisation at a high temperature to destroy the enzymes and micro-organisms. A vacuum is formed by the lid preventing the re-entry of air and micro-organisms into the jar.

Note: The bottling of fish, meat, poultry and vegetables at home is not recommended.

BASIC GUIDELINES

- Choose suitable fruits which are in perfect condition
- Clean jars, lids and rings by washing in hot water
- Do not dry jars, leave wet inside, sterilise in the oven
- Prepare fruit according to kind, pack into jars, close to top
- Prepare syrup, boil for 5 minutes
- Pour syrup over fruit in jar ensuring that no air bubbles form
- Place ring and cover on jar, apply band, screw tightly and unscrew to allow steam to escape and a vacuum to form during processing
- Sterilise the produce in a pressure cooker, in a saucepan on the hob or in oven
- Remove and tighten screw band to ensure that a vacuum forms
- Cool and tighten band again, test seal after 12 hours, and label
- Store in a dry, dark, well ventilated cupboard in a cool area

FREEZING

UNDERLYING PRINCIPLE

Freezing involves the removal of warmth and moisture. This inactivates enzymes and micro-organisms. Water is converted into small ice crystals by *quick freezing* ($-25°C$) and large ice crystals by *slow freezing* ($-15°C$ to $0°C$). Frozen foods are stored at $-18°C$.

ADVANTAGES OF FREEZING

- Great variety of foods can be frozen
- Bulk freezing saves fuel and time
- Foods available out of season

- Little waste during preparation
- Food can be frozen in useable quantities
- Colour, flavours and nutritive value retained

DISADVANTAGES OF FREEZING

- Freezers are expensive to buy
- Texture changes and freezer burn
- Packaging and running costs
- Keeping the freezer filled

EXAMPLES OF FOODS FOR FREEZING

Cooked and fresh meats, poultry, fish, sauces, soups, fresh fruits, vegetables, uncooked doughs and pastries, breadcrumbs, breads, cakes, pastries, cooked sweet and savoury dishes.

SOME FOODS UNSUITABLE FOR FREEZING

Bananas, salad vegetables, whole pears, melons, whole tomatoes, whole eggs, dairy produce, mayonnaise, foods with high fat or water content.

FREEZER PACKAGING

Polythene boxes and bags, waxed cartons and tubs, freezer foil, freezer tape, coated wire ties, foil containers. All containers must be moisture proof.

GENERAL GUIDELINES FOR FREEZING

- Choose fresh, high quality foods
- Turn freezer to coldest setting, 3 hours beforehand
- Divide food into useable quantities
- Prepare, pack and label correctly
- Use extra foil over sharp bones on meat
- Allow head space over liquids for expansion
- Freeze in the fast freeze section
- Open freeze foods that would stick together
- Store same type foods together
- Keep a list of what is in the freezer
- Use in rotation

RULES FOR THAWING FOOD

- Thaw foods completely
- Thoroughly cook all thawed foods
- Never refreeze frozen foods
- Use foods within the recommended time
- Cook vegetables from frozen
- Use thawed foods quickly

FREEZER BURN

Protein foods exposed in the freezer will toughen and discolour e.g. if wrapper is torn. This is freezer burn.

BLANCHING

Vegetables are blanched or dipped in boiling salted water before freezing for a short time to destroy the enzymes.

JAM MAKING AND JELLIES

UNDERLYING PRINCIPLE

Fruits are boiled to 100°C, in the presence of sugar, to destroy the enzymes and micro-organisms present.

PECTIN

Pectin is a polysaccharide present in cell walls of fruit. It ensures that jams and jellies set. The use of an acid helps draw out the pectin from the cell walls. The proportions of pectin, acid and sugar determine the setting quality of jams and jellies. The stage of maturity of the fruit influences the amount of pectin present. Under-ripe or over-ripe fruits will not set.

Fruit	Contains	Setting quality
Unripe fruits	Pectose	Poor
Ripe fruits	Pectin	Good
Over-ripe fruit	Pectic acid	Poor

Crystallisation results when too little sugar is used
Fermentation results when too much sugar is used

TEST FOR PECTIN

Take a small sample of the fruit, boil and remove one teaspoon of the fruit juice. Mix into three teaspoons of methylated spirits and cool slightly. The fruit juice will react with the methylated spirits.

Results

High in pectin —> Large single clot
Average pectin —> Two soft clots
Poor in pectin —> Numerous clots

GENERAL GUIDELINES FOR JAM-MAKING

- Choose large stainless steel saucepan
- Jars should be perfect, without chips or flaws
- Clean jars thoroughly, sterilise in oven for 15 minutes
- Select sound fruit
- Prepare fruit according to kind (Specify details in exam)
- Depending on fruit type, add a little water to soften the fruit
- Warm sugar, add to softened fruit and dissolve thoroughly
- Bring to boil, test frequently for setting point, boil rapidly until set, remove scum by skimming jam, do not stir
- Remove from heat, pour into pre-heated sterilised jars filling close to the top, wipe rims and cover
- Label, cool and store in a dark, dry, well-ventilated cupboard

THE THREE SETTING TESTS

Temperature Test

Using a warmed sugar thermometer, check the jam until it reaches the setting point of 104°C.

Cold Plate Test

As the jam is cooking, remove a small quantity with a spoon, pour onto a cold plate and cool. If the surface of the jam sample wrinkles when the plate is tilted, setting point has been reached.

Flake Test

Using a wooden spoon take a spoon of jam, cool slightly and pour the jam off the spoon. Setting point has been reached if the jam falls off in one flake. Jam pouring off the spoon indicates that it needs more cooking.

COMMERCIAL PRESERVATION

Commercial preservation includes bottling, canning, dehydration and freezing.

BOTTLING AND CANNING

Bottled and canned foods are easy to transport and store. Similar to home bottling and canning except for the scale of production and the ultra-high temperatures involved. All types of foods are used in commercial bottling and canning.

UNDERLYING PRINCIPLE

Bottling and canning involve ultra-high temperatures which destroy enzymes and micro-organisms. Following sterilisation, cans are sealed hermetically to make them airtight and to prevent the re-entry of micro-organisms.

Aseptic canning involves sterilising the cans and the foods separately at ultra-high temperatures, reducing the loss of colour, flavour, nutrients and texture.

CHEMICAL PRESERVATION

Similar to home preservation. Salt, smoking, sugar and vinegar are used. Foods include chutneys, jams, jellies, marmalade, pickles, cured and salted meats, salted vegetables and smoked fish.

DEHYDRATION

UNDERLYING PRINCIPLE

Moisture is removed from the cells in food and salt and sugar concentrations increase. This ensures that the micro-organisms cannot multiply as the moisture is removed from their cell walls in the drying process.

METHODS OF DEHYDRATION

Accelerated Freeze Drying (AFD)

Food undergoes quick freezing at $-30°C$ and then the drying process changes the ice crystals by sublimation to a vapour on becoming a liquid. Foods rehydrate quickly. Little loss of nutrients.

Air Drying

Foods undergo preparation, sometimes blanching and pass through hot air tunnels until the moisture level is reduced to 5–10%.

Puff Drying
Prepared food is dried in a vacuum chamber to reduce the moisture by 70%. The remaining 30% moisture in the food expands under reduced air pressure. The process continues until the moisture content has been reduced to 5%.

Roller Drying
Prepared food is poured over revolving heated drums or rollers, dries and is scraped off in powder or flakes. Examples of foods: milk and potatoes.

Spray Drying
The food is sprayed into a heated chamber and dehydrates as it falls to the bottom of the chamber as droplets or powder. Examples of foods: eggs and milk.

COMMERCIAL FREEZING

Commercial freezing is carried out at very low temperature, -30°C, resulting in small ice crystals. The product produced is as near as possible to the nutritive value, colour flavour and texture of the fresh food.

AIR BLAST FREEZING
Cold air at -30°C is used to freeze food as it is blown over it.

CONTACT OR PLATE FREEZING
Food is arranged on refrigerated shelves and the food freezes in a short time due to contact with the shelves.

CRYOGENIC FREEZING
Liquid nitrogen is used to freeze foods in a short time e.g. prawns.

FLOW FREEZING
Cold air at -30°C is blown under foods e.g. berries, corn, peas, to prevent them sticking together as they move on a conveyor belt.

SPRAY FREEZING
Prepared food is sprayed with freezing liquid brine or syrup before it is packed.

IMMERSION FREEZING
Large foods are immersed in freezing brine and then packed e.g. meats, poultry. All traces of the brine or syrup are removed before packing.

IRRADIATION

Fruits and vegetables are sterilised using ionising radiation to delay ripening, destroy micro-organisms, kill insects and prevent sprouting.

8

HUMAN PHYSIOLOGY

BODY CELLS AND TISSUES

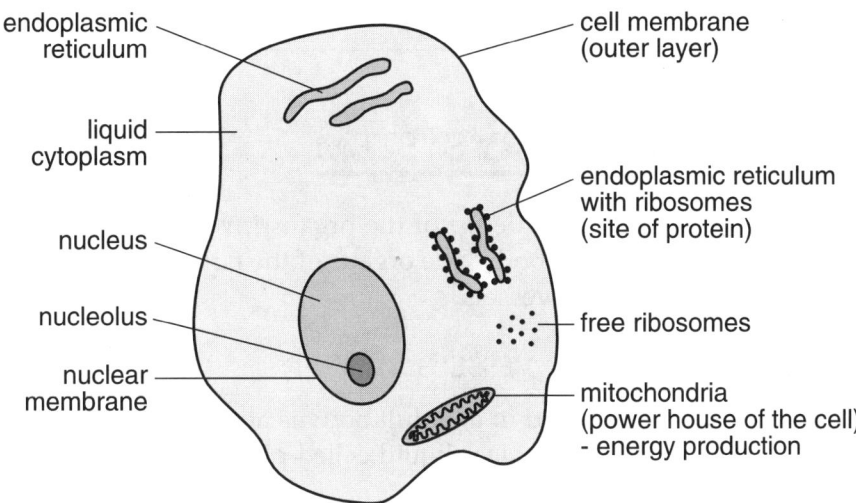

A basic cell is composed of an outer layer or cell membrane, a nucleus, endoplasmic reticulum, Golgi apparatus, mitochondria, ribosomes and vacuoles suspended in the cytoplasm.

The body consists of cells varying in shape, size, structure and function. Cells which have the same function, group together to form tissues. Tissues group together to form organs. Organs group to form body systems.

EXAMPLES OF CELLS
Blood cells (red, white), liver, muscle, nerve, skin and sperm cells

Tissue types	Locations within the body
Connective	
Adipose	Under skin, around organs
Blood	Fluid tissue in the circulatory system
Bone	Bones
Cartilage	Ends of bones, ears, nose
Elastic	Walls of blood vessels, lungs
Ligaments	Muscles
Epithelial	Skin, lining membranes
Nervous	Nervous system, brain, spinal cord
Muscle	
Cardiac	Heart walls
Skeletal	Skeletal muscles
Smooth	Internal organs, blood vessels

THE CIRCULATORY SYSTEM

The circulatory system is made up of the organs involved in transporting or pumping blood around the body. The organs of the circulatory system include the heart, blood and blood vessels.

THE BLOOD AND BLOOD VESSELS

The average volume of blood in an adult body is about 5 litres. Blood consists of cells (45%) suspended in a clear liquid called plasma (55%).

COMPOSITION OF BLOOD
Blood consists of:
- Red cells or Erythrocytes
- White cells or Leucocytes
- Platelets or Thrombocytes

Plasma consists of:
- Water
- Plasma proteins: albumin, globulin, fibrinogen, clotting factors
- Inorganic salts: sodium chloride, sodium bicarbonate

- Nutrient material: amino acids, fatty acids and glycerol etc.
- Organic wastes: urea, uric acid
- Hormones
- Antibodies
- Enzymes
- Gases: oxygen, carbon dioxide, nitrogen

BLOOD CELLS: KEY POINTS TO NOTE
Erythrocytes or Red Cells
- Soft, flexible circular biconcave discs
- No nucleus
- Formed in bone marrow and spleen
- Contain haemoglobin that combines with oxygen
- Live for about 4 months
- Require iron

Leucocytes or White Cells
- Larger than red cells, irregular in shape and fewer in number
- Each possesses a nucleus
- No haemoglobin
- Formed in the bone marrow, lymph nodes and the spleen
- Life span of about 14 days
- Two types: *phagocytes* surround, engulf and destroy invading bodies (bacteria, viruses) and *lymphocytes* are involved in the production of antibodies

Thrombocytes or Platelets
- Smallest of the blood cells
- No nucleus
- Help blood to clot
- Formed in the bone marrow
- Last about 4 days

SUMMARY OF THE FUNCTIONS OF BLOOD
- Regulates body temperature by distributing heat around the body
- Transports nutrients, water, enzymes, hormones and oxygen
- Haemoglobin absorbs oxygen in the lungs and brings it to cells
- Collects and transports carbon dioxide to the lungs for the exchange of gases

- Collects urea and brings it to the kidneys for removal
- Maintains a balanced environment in the blood i.e. homeostasis
- Protects the body against diseases and infections

CLOTTING OF BLOOD
Following a cut or an injury, blood clots form and seal the wound preventing infections and disease. This happens when:
- Injured cells and platelets release thromboplastin
- Thromboplastin converts prothrombin to thrombin
- Thrombin causes soluble fibrinogen to form insoluble fibrin
- A clot or network forms, traps red cells and platelets, seals the injury
- Bleeding stops and a hard scab forms protecting the new cells underneath

BLOOD VESSELS
Three types of blood vessels transport the blood around the body.

Arteries
- Have elastic, thick walls with three layers and a small lumen
- Carry blood away from the heart
- Carry bright red oxygenated blood, except for pulmonary artery
- Do not have valves
- Arteries branch into arterioles, arterioles form smaller capillaries

Capillaries
- Small, thin, single-walled blood vessels made from endothelial cells
- Link arteries and veins
- Help the blood to perform its function of nutrient–waste exchange
- Allow for the exchange of nutrients, gases (O_2, CO_2) and waste products
- Capillaries join to form venules, venules form veins

Veins
- Contain most of the blood in the body
- Thinner walls than arteries with three main layers
- Larger lumen than arteries
- Return blood to the heart
- Carry deoxygenated blood, except for pulmonary veins
- Contain valves, which prevent backward flow of blood

Blood Groups

Blood can be classified into four groups, A, B, AB and O, according to the antigen present in the red blood cells. Antibodies, present in plasma, and antigens determine which blood groups are compatible. Recipient's blood must not contain antibodies that will react with the antigens in the donor's cells. A reaction results in agglutination i.e. clumping of red blood cells.

Blood group	Antigens	Antibodies	Donate to	Receive from
O	None	Anti-A and anti-B	All groups	O only
A	A	Anti-B	A, AB	Groups A and O
B	B	Anti-A	B, AB	Groups B and O
AB	A, B	None	AB	All groups

Blood group O is known as the *universal donor*. It can be donated to all blood groups.

Blood group AB is known as the *universal recipient*. It can receive blood from all groups.

Rhesus Factor

Eighty-five percent of the population have another antigen present called the Rhesus factor (Rh+). Those without the Rhesus antigen are said to be Rhesus negative (Rh–). It can become a problem during pregnancy. If a Rh–ve mother delivers a Rh+ve baby a small number of Rh+ve bodies cross through the placenta and enter her blood stream during childbirth or in late pregnancy resulting in the formation of antibodies. These antibodies could cause agglutination in subsequent babies. This can now be avoided with correct medical intervention.

THE HEART

Position, Shape and Size

- Located behind the sternum, to the left of centre, between the left and right lungs, above the diaphragm
- Protected by the sternum and the rib cage
- A pear-shaped organ composed of branching fibres of cardiac muscle
- The apex points downwards and the wider end is at the top
- Is like a pump, circulating the blood around the body
- About the size of a clenched fist

Structure
- Outer layer of tissue consisting of pericardium, myocardium and endocardium
- Two upper chambers composed of thin-walled atria or auricles which receive blood from veins into the heart
- Two lower chambers composed of thick muscular walled ventricles which pump blood into arteries out of the heart
- Valves separate the atria or auricles from the ventricles:
  tricuspid valve separates right auricle from right ventricle
  bicuspid or mitral valve separate left auricle from left ventricle
- Wall of the left ventricle is thicker than the wall of the right ventricle
- Dividing or central wall of the heart, the septum
- Pericardium, a moist smooth membrane, surrounds and protects the heart

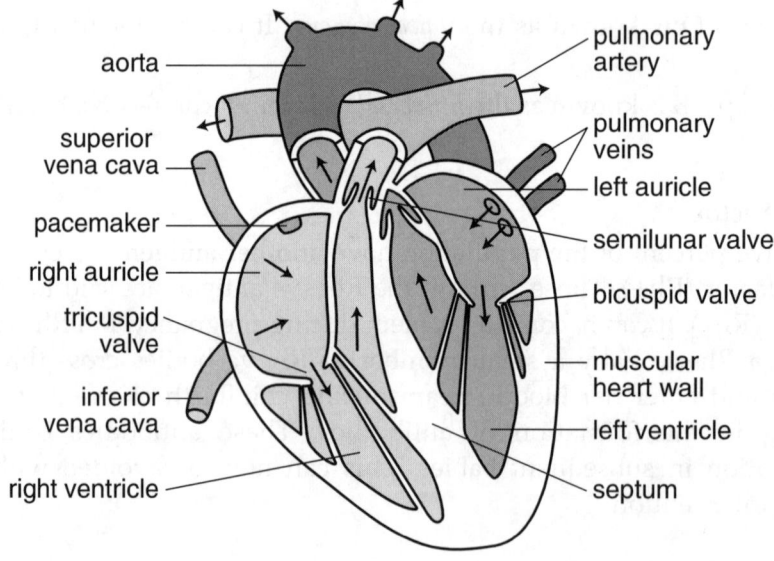

Blood Vessels Connected to the Heart
The blood vessels connected to the heart are the superior and inferior venae cavae, pulmonary artery, pulmonary veins, aorta and the coronary arteries.

Summary of the Pulmonary Circulation
The blood flows in one direction only, through the heart to the lungs, purified in the lungs and returned to the heart. The stages involved are:

- *De-oxygenated blood*, from body tissues, enters the right auricle via the superior and inferior venae cavae. The right auricle pumps de-oxygenated blood into the right ventricle through the tricuspid valve. The blood is pumped by the contraction of the ventricle wall through semi-lunar valves into the pulmonary artery. The pulmonary artery brings the blood to the lungs to be purified.
- *Oxygenated blood* returns to the heart via the pulmonary veins and enters the left auricle. From the left auricle, oxygenated blood is pumped into the left ventricle through the mitral valve or bicuspid valve. The walls of the left ventricle contract pumping the blood through semilunar valves into the aorta which transports the purified or oxygenated blood to the rest of the body.

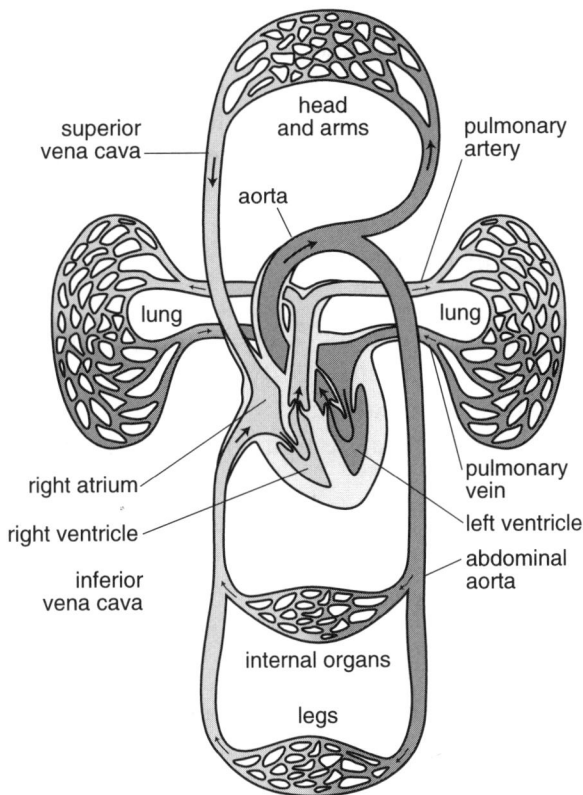

SUMMARY OF THE SYSTEMIC CIRCULATION

The *aorta* divides into arteries outside the heart. Oxygenated blood is transported to the upper and lower parts of the body. Arteries branch into arterioles and eventually form capillaries. Through the network of capillaries oxygen and nutrients are exchanged for waste products. Oxygen is exchanged in the cells for carbon dioxide.

Capillaries unite to form veins that bring the de-oxygenated dark red or impure blood to the superior and inferior venae cava which empty into the right auricle. The pulmonary circulation begins again.

THE CARDIAC CYCLE OR HEARTBEAT
Cardiac muscle contracts and relaxes during heartbeat. Contraction is referred to as systole and relaxation is referred to as diastole. Systole is followed by diastole. Auricles and ventricles are relaxed during diastole.

THE RHYTHM OF THE HEART
The rhythm of the heart is controlled by muscle cells, which are called the pacemaker. The pacemaker is located in the wall of the auricle. It creates electrical impulses that stimulate the auricles to contract. These impulses are relayed, and the atrio-ventricular node reacts causing the muscles in the walls of the ventricles to contract. The frequency of the heartbeat averages around 72 beats per minute.

Factors influencing Rate of Heartbeat
- Medulla oblongata
- Different levels of activity e.g. relaxing, running, swimming, walking
- Age and body size (baby, adult, elderly)
- Drugs, depressants and stimulants
- Emotions, excitement and fear, 'prepare for fight or flight'

Pulse
This is the rate of blood flow corresponding to beating of the heart.
Average pulse rate=72 beats per minute

Factors affecting Blood Pressure
The factors are exercise, general health, sleep, ageing (in some cases), emotional wellbeing, rate of flow of the blood and the resistance to its flow.

Measuring Blood Pressure
The flow of blood through the circulatory system exerts pressure on the walls of the blood vessels. Blood pressure is expressed as 120/80, where 120 represents systolic blood pressure and 80 represents diastolic blood pressure. Measurements are in millimetres of mercury.

THE DIGESTIVE SYSTEM

During digestion food is broken down from large insoluble molecules into small soluble molecules that can be absorbed and used by the body.

DIGESTION OCCURS IN TWO STAGES

Mechanical or physical: food is physically broken down by the action of the teeth (chewing, grinding), churning action in the stomach and peristaltic movement of the digestive system.

Chemical: enzymes cause chemical reactions with substances in food during the mechanical process, reducing them to simpler substances which can be easily absorbed.

STRUCTURE

The digestive system is composed of:
- The *alimentary canal*, a continuous muscular tube extending from the mouth to the anus, consisting of the mouth, oesophagus, stomach, small intestine, large intestine, rectum and anus.
- Other organs involved in the process are: salivary glands, liver, gall bladder and pancreas.

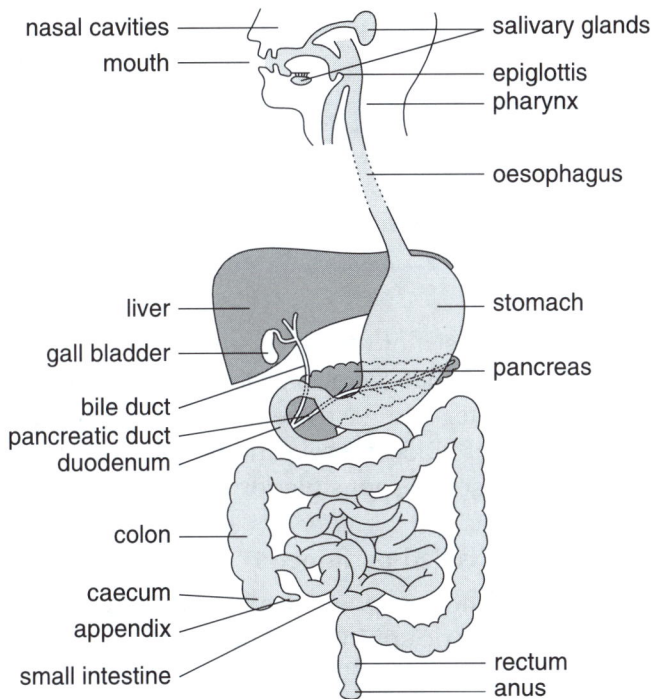

The Mouth
- Food is reduced by the grinding and chewing action of the teeth
- Surface area of food increases and saliva from the three salivary glands moistens it
- Saliva is secreted by the paratoid gland, submaxillary gland and sublingual gland
- Food forms a ball or bolus

Digestion in the mouth: cooked starch is converted to dextrin by the enzyme ptyalin.

The Oesophagus
- Food passes from the mouth to the oesophagus, a muscular tube about 25 cm in length
- Peristaltic waves move food along the oesophagus down into the stomach
- The oesophagus enters the stomach at the cardiac end. The cardiac sphincter controls entry of food into the stomach, preventing regurgitation of food back into the oesophagus

Digestion in the oesophagus: no enzymes are secreted in the oesophagus. The action of ptyalin on cooked starch, begun in the mouth, continues.

The Stomach
Position
Located just below the diaphragm to the top left side of the abdomen, in front of the pancreas and to the left of the liver.

Shape
A large hollow sac or organ.

Structure
The walls of the stomach consist of four layers:
- An inner mucous layer that secretes gastric juice consisting of mucus, hydrochloric acid, water and gastric enzymes, pepsinogen and rennin
- A sub-mucous layer of blood vessels and nerves
- Layers of smooth muscle responsible for the churning of food in the stomach
- A smooth outer layer called peritoneum

The cardiac sphincter is at the oesophagus end, and the pyloric sphincter is at the duodenum end. The pyloric sphincter controls the exit of chyme from the stomach into the duodenum.

Action in the Stomach
- Food stays in the stomach for approximately 2–5 hours
- Food is churned about, broken down and mixed with gastric juice, forms chyme
- Food passes from the stomach to the duodenum of the small intestine

Digestion in the Stomach
- Involves physical and chemical processes
- Hydrochloric acid converts pepsinogen which converts to the enzyme pepsin
- Pepsin converts proteins to polypeptides
- Rennin converts caseinogen (milk protein) to casein

Absorption in the Stomach
Limited absorption of alcohol, water and some fat-soluble drugs

THE SMALL INTESTINE
- Links the stomach with the large intestine (about 6–8 metres in length)
- Consists of duodenum, jejunum and ileum

The walls of the small intestine are composed of a deeply folded inner mucous layer, a sub-mucous layer, a smooth muscle layer and an outer layer of peritoneum. The inner mucous layer is covered with villi, each with a lacteal and a network of capillaries. Glands between the villi secrete intestinal juices containing enzymes.

Digestion in the Small Intestine
Chyme entering the duodenum is mixed with duodenal secretions, bile and pancreatic juice. The intestinal juice of the small intestine produces the enzymes erepsin, lactase, maltase and sucrase.

Action in the Duodenum

Enzymes	Works on:	Converts to:
Amylase	Starch	Maltose (sugars)
Lipase	Fats	Fatty acids and glycerol
Trypsin	Large protein molecules	Peptone

Action in the Jejunum

Enzymes	Works on:	Converts to:
Erepsin	Partly digested proteins	Amino acids

Disaccharides are broken down into monosaccharides:
- Lactase works on lactose and converts it to glucose and galactose
- Maltase works on maltose and converts it to glucose
- Sucrase works on sucrose and converts it to glucose and fructose

Remaining Lipids
Lipase works on any remaining lipids breaking them into fatty acids and glycerol.

Action in the Ileum
- Amino acids and monosaccharides are absorbed and transported to the liver
- Glycerol and fatty acids diffuse into the lacteals, convert into lipids and are transported by the lymph system to the left subclavian vein
- Substances not absorbed pass into the large intestine

Absorption in the Small Intestine
Amino acids, glucose, some mineral salts and water-soluble vitamins are absorbed through the capillaries into the bloodstream. Emulsified fats and fat-soluble vitamins, vitamins A and D, are absorbed into the lacteals and are transported by the lymph vessels to the thoracic duct.

THE LARGE INTESTINE
The large intestine is like a tube about 2 metres long. It consists of the caecum, appendix, ascending, transverse and descending colon and rectum. Chyme moves from the ileum into the caecum. Peristaltic wave-like movements move the digested food along the colon to the rectum. Faeces, the solid waste, is eliminated through the anus by the contractions of the anal sphincter.

Absorption in the Large Intestine
By the time digested food reaches the ileum, digestion is almost complete. In the ileum, any undigested food is acted on by the succus entericus. Vitamin B and K, produced by the bacteria present, remaining minerals and water from the digested food are re-absorbed.

Summary of Digestion and Absorption of Nutrients
Proteins
Digestion of Proteins

Organ	Digestive juice	Enzymes and action
Mouth	Saliva	No action on protein
Stomach	Gastric juice	Pepsin converts all proteins to polypeptides
Small intestine	Pancreatic juice	Trypsin converts polypeptides to di- and tri-peptides
	In microvilli	Peptidase converts peptides to amino acids

Absorption of Proteins
Amino acids are absorbed into the villi of the small intestine and transported to the liver via the portal circulation.

Carbohydrates
Digestion of Carbohydrates

Organ	Digestive juice	Enzymes and action
Mouth	Saliva	Amylase converts cooked starch to dextrin
Stomach	Gastric juice	Hydrochloric acid stops the action of amylase
Small intestine	Pancreatic juice	Amylase converts all starches to disaccharides
	In the villi	Lactase, maltase and sucrase convert sugars to monosaccharides

Absorption of Carbohydrates
Glucose is absorbed into the villi and transported to the liver via the portal circulation.

Lipids

Digestion of Lipids

Organ	Digestive juice	Enzymes and action
Mouth	Saliva	No action on lipids
Stomach	Gastric juice	No action on lipids
Small intestine	Bile	Bile emulsifies fats
	Pancreatic juice	Lipase converts fats to glycerol and fatty acids
	In the villi	Lipase completes the digestion of fats

Absorption of Lipids

Glycerol and fatty acids are absorbed into the lacteals of the villi. They are transported to the left subclavian vein.

THE PANCREAS

POSITION AND SHAPE

The pancreas, a long gland, is located under the stomach, stretching from the spleen to the duodenum.

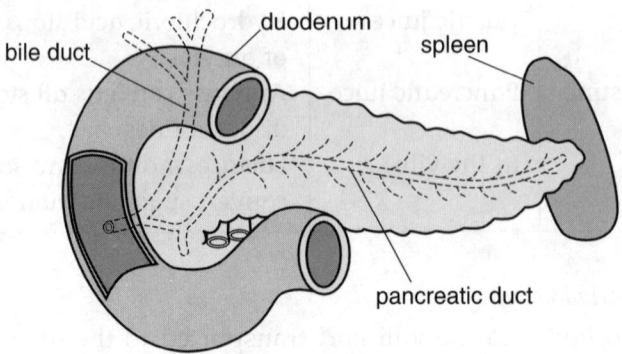

STRUCTURE

Made up of secretory cells, alveoli, and the Islets of Langerhans (produce insulin). It is both an exocrine and endocrine gland.

FUNCTION

Secretes pancreatic juice and releases it with the enzymes trypsin, amylase and lipase into the duodenum.

BILE

Bile is produced in the liver and stored in the gall bladder. The gall bladder releases bile, a greenish alkaline fluid, through the bile duct onto the chyme in the duodenum. Bile reacts with fats, breaking them down into an emulsion.

THE LIVER

Position

Lies near the stomach, above the small intestine, directly under the diaphragm and occupies the top right corner of the abdominal cavity.

SHAPE AND COLOUR

A triangular-shaped, dark-coloured organ.

STRUCTURE

- Covered by peritoneum, has two lobes, one larger than the other
- Portal vein brings blood, rich in nutrients, from the digestive system to the liver
- Hepatic artery supplies oxygenated blood
- Hepatic vein brings deoxygenated blood away from the liver, drains into inferior vena cava
- Hepatic ducts bring bile away from the liver to the duodenum

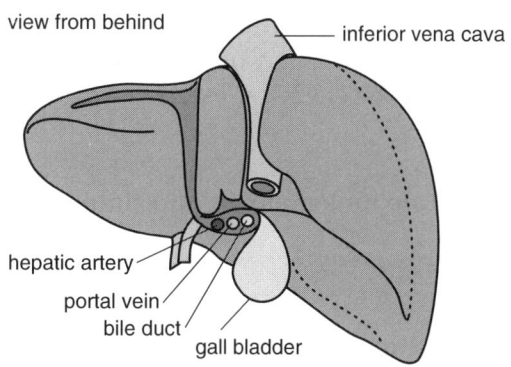

LIVER LOBULES

The liver consists of lobules made up of groups of liver cells arranged in columns around a central vein. A branch of the hepatic artery brings oxygenated blood to the liver and the hepatic portal vein brings nutrient-rich blood. Deoxygenated blood is taken away by the hepatic vein. Between the liver cells, bile is secreted and emptied into hepatic ducts. Bile from the liver is transported to the duodenum via the bile duct. Excess bile is stored in the gall bladder.

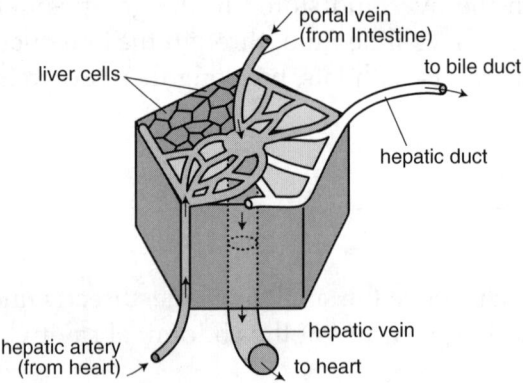

SUMMARY OF LIVER FUNCTIONS

- Converts glucose into glycogen, stored for later use
- Assists in the secretion of bile, emulsifies fats
- Deamination of amino acids
- Synthesis of antibodies and plasma proteins
- Filters and breaks down toxins e.g. poisons, drugs
- Stores nutrients e.g. fat-soluble vitamins, iron
- Completes the breakdown of red blood cells

METABOLISM

A variety of chemical processes takes place in the body to ensure that food is converted into substances that can be used within the body. Metabolism involves the digestion and absorption of food, storage and use of nutrients within the body. It involves the chemical reactions, catabolism and anabolism.

CATABOLISM

Larger molecules in food are broken down into simpler molecules and energy is released.

ANABOLISM

Energy is used when smaller molecules are combined to build complex molecules.

METABOLISM OF PROTEINS

The portal vein brings amino acids to the liver. Most are passed into the bloodstream and body tissues where they are used for growth and repair of cells, and the manufacture of enzymes and hormones. Excess amino acids are deaminated.

METABOLISM OF CARBOHYDRATES

On reaching the liver, monosaccharides are converted to glucose. Some are converted into glycogen and others released into the bloodstream for energy. Excess glucose is converted to fat and stored as adipose tissue.

METABOLISM OF LIPIDS

Some lipids on reaching the liver are converted into energy. Excess lipid is converted into adipose tissue and stored under the skin. This is an energy store within the body.

THE ENDOCRINE SYSTEM

The endocrine system maintains homeostasis by releasing hormones and controls processes such as development, reproduction and metabolism.

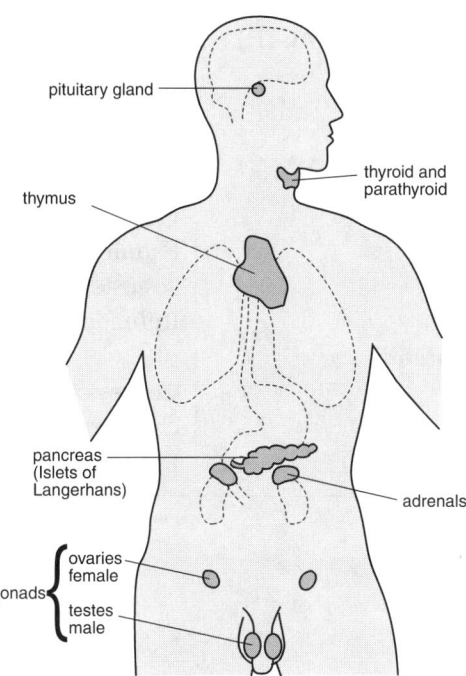

THE ENDOCRINE SYSTEM CONSISTS OF

Exocrine or ducted glands: secretions pass down a duct to the site where action is demanded e.g. salivary glands

Endocrine or ductless glands: secretions pass directly into the bloodstream and have a more widespread effect than exocrine secretions

MAIN ENDOCRINE GLANDS

Pituitary, thyroid, parathyroid, adrenals, Islets of Langerhans (in the pancreas) and gonads (ovaries in females, testes in males)

THE PITUITARY GLAND
- Lies at the base of the brain, consists of two sections, anterior and posterior pituitary, and controls output of other endocrine glands by a feedback system.

SUMMARY OF HORMONES AND FUNCTIONS

Gland	Functions
Anterior pituitary gland	
Thyroid-stimulating hormone (TSH)	Thyroid secretion of thyroxine
Growth-stimulating hormone (HGH)	Regulates growth of cells
Melanocyte-stimulating hormone (MSH)	Influences skin pigmentation
Adrenocorticotropic hormone (ACTH)	Causes release of hormones from adrenal cortex
Follicle-stimulating hormone (FSH)	Oestrogen production and ripening of ovum (affects sperm production in males)
Luteinising hormone (LH)	Progesterone production in females
	Testosterone production in males
Lactogenic hormone	Influences lactation
Posterior pituitary gland	
Oxytocin	Causes contractions during childbirth
Antidiuretic hormone (ADH)	Influences water balance in urine

OTHER ENDOCRINE GLANDS

Glands	Hormone	Effects
Thyroid	Thyroxin	Stimulates metabolism
		Reduces blood calcium levels
Parathyroid	Parathormone	Raises blood calcium levels
Islets of Langerhans	Insulin	Balances blood sugar levels
Adrenal glands	Adrenalin	Raises blood sugar level
		Increases rate of heartbeat, blood pressure
	Noradrenaline	Maintenance of blood pressure
	Aldosterone	Controls salt/water balance
	Glucocorticoids	Regulates metabolism
		Regulates storage of glycogen in the liver
		Decreases anxiety and stress
Gonads		
Ovaries (female)	Oestrogen	Controls secondary characteristics
		Regulates ovulation
	Progesterone	Promotes growth of uterine lining
Testes (male)	Testosterone	Controls secondary characteristics
		Assists sperm production

THYMUS GLAND

The thymus gland lies behind the sternum, in front of the lungs and the heart and extends upwards into the root of the neck. The thymus gland plays an important part in the development of the lymphatic system. It grows until puberty but its effectiveness declines with increasing age.

DISORDERS ASSOCIATED WITH THE ENDOCRINE SYSTEM

Hyposecretion disorders result from deficiency of a particular hormone
Hypersecretion disorders result from the overproduction of a hormone

THYROXINE

Deficiency: reduced metabolic rate, obesity, goitre, dwarfism
Excess: increased metabolism, weight loss, sweating, giantism

PARATHORMONE
Deficiency: 'pins and needles', muscular spasm, convulsions
Excess: raised blood calcium, weak bones, kidney stones

INSULIN
Deficiency: increase in blood sugar, glucose in urine, diabetes mellitus
Excess: low blood sugar, can result in coma

FEEDBACK SYSTEM

Endocrine glands secrete hormones as they are required. A self-regulating feed-back system controls the amount of hormones secreted by the endocrine glands to achieve a correct balance within the body.

THE LYMPHATIC SYSTEM

POSITION

The lymphatic system acts as a medium of exchange or a bridge between the cells and the blood. It allows nutrients and oxygen to transfer from the blood to the cells, and for urea and carbon dioxide to transfer from the cells to the blood.

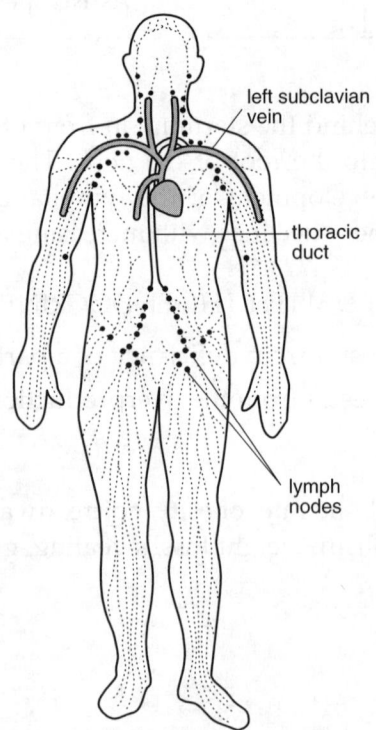

STRUCTURE

The lymphatic system consists of lymph fluid, lymph vessels and lymph nodes. The spleen and thymus gland play a part in the development of the lymphatic system during embryonic life and early childhood. A colourless fluid called lymph is carried in the lymph system. Lymph flows in one direction only. The structure of lymph vessels is similar to that of veins.

LYMPH VESSELS
- Blind-ended ducts located between the cells
- Join together to form larger lymphatics or lymph vessels
- Similar to veins but with thin walls
- Pass through lymph nodes
- Have valves to prevent the lymph flowing backwards

LACTEALS
- Located in the villi of the small intestine
- Absorb and return regulated amounts of digested fats to the blood stream

LYMPH NODES
- Consist of connective tissue
- Located at intervals along the lymph vessels
- Found in the abdomen, armpits, chest, neck and groin
- Act as a filter system with special cells for fighting infections and foreign bodies
- Produce lymphocytes

FORMATION OF LYMPH: THE FLUID

A little plasma diffuses through the walls of the blood capillaries into the spaces between the cells forming tissue fluid or extra-cellular fluid (ECF). This fluid, containing oxygen and nutrients, surrounds the cells. The oxygen and nutrients diffuse through the walls of the cells replacing the carbon dioxide and urea released into the extra-cellular fluid.

Some of the excess ECF returns to the blood stream. The remaining fluid drains into the lymph capillaries, located between the cells, and is now referred to as lymph. Lymph travels through the lymph system, drains into the thoracic duct and returns to the blood stream at the left subclavian vein.

FUNCTIONS OF THE LYMPH SYSTEM

- Acts as a bridge between the blood and the cells
- Returns excess tissue fluid to the blood
- Drains the tissue spaces by collecting lymph, including plasma
- Returns plasma proteins to the blood
- Absorbs and transports digested fats
- Manufactures lymphocytes which produce antibodies
- Localises infections and prevents their spread
- Re-circulates urea and carbon dioxide for excretion

THE SPLEEN

POSITION

Lies below the diaphragm, to the left of the abdomen, near the stomach, left kidney and pancreas.

SHAPE AND STRUCTURE

- Bean-shaped organ
- Consists of spongy tissue
- Splenic artery supplies spleen with blood

GENERAL FUNCTIONS OF THE SPLEEN

- Filters worn-out red blood cells for recycling
- Forms new red blood cells in the foetus
- Filters and destroys bacteria in the blood
- Produces lymphocytes
- Acts as a blood reservoir (used in emergencies)

THE NERVOUS SYSTEM

The nervous system controls co-ordination and communication within the body. It functions in two ways, voluntary and involuntary.

The nervous system is divided into:

Central nervous system (CNS): brain (cerebrum, cerebellum, medulla oblongata), brain stem and spinal cord

Peripheral Nervous System: cranial nerve fibres and spinal nerve fibres

Autonomic Nervous System: sympathetic nervous system and the parasympathetic nervous system

NERVES

- Consist of both motor and sensory neurons
- Enclosed by a protective layer of connective tissue
- Produce nerve impulses

NEURONS

Neurons are the basis cells of the nervous system. Neurons are made up of cell bodies with nuclei surrounded by protoplasm, cell membranes and nerve fibres called axons and dendrites. The nerve fibres are filled with protoplasm and protected by cell membranes.

TYPES OF NEURONS

MOTOR OR EFFERENT NEURONS

- Carry impulses away from the CNS to the muscles and glands of the body
- Consist of an irregular cell body, dendrites, axon and end plate attached to muscle

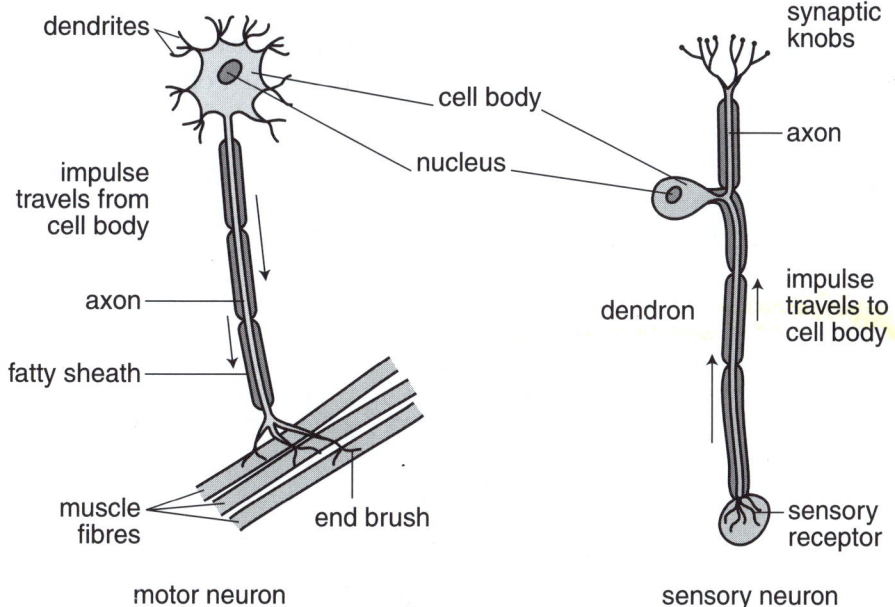

SENSORY OR AFFERENT NEURONS
- Carry impulses from the body to the spinal cord. The impulses may then pass to the brain or to connector neurons of reflex arcs in the spinal cord.
- Consist of sensory receptor, dendron, cell body, axon, synaptic knobs

ASSOCIATION OR CONNECTOR NEURONS
- Link the activities of the motor and sensory neurons
- Lie in the brain and spinal cord

THE TRANSMISSION OF NERVE IMPULSES: SYNAPSES

Synapses are the junctions at which nerve impulses are transmitted between neurons.

When a nerve impulse arrives at the end of the axon a chemical substance, acetylcholine (ACh), is released. It diffuses across each synapse transmitting the impulse to the nearby dendrites of the next neuron.

NERVE IMPULSES

Nerve impulses require oxygen, produce electrochemical impulses which cause chemical transmissions between neurons, motor neurons and effectors.

THE CENTRAL NERVOUS SYSTEM

THE BRAIN

The brain is protected by the skull and surrounded by the meninges. It consists of the cerebrum, midbrain, pons, cerebellum and medulla oblongata.

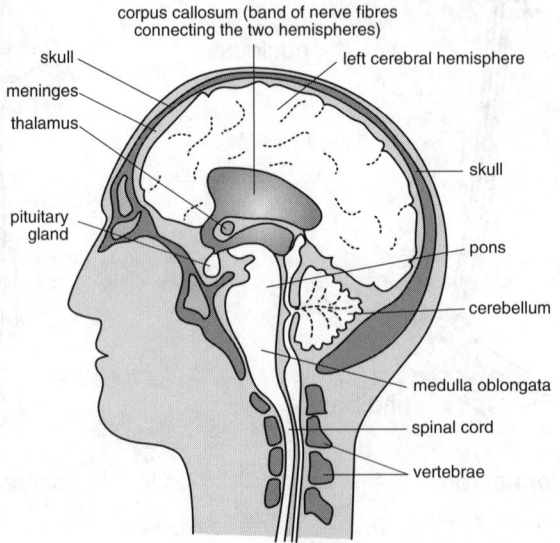

The Cerebrum

This is the largest area of the brain, lying in the forebrain and consisting of the right and left hemispheres. Millions of nerve cells are tightly packed into the grey matter of the outer cerebral cortex. Nerve fibres in the white matter beneath the grey area link the nerve cells of the cortex to the brain stem. Areas within the cerebrum control specific actions.

Cerebral Cortex
Controls: mental activities e.g. memory, sensory perception, and initiation and control of voluntary muscle contractions

Hypothalamus
Controls: body temperature, hunger, thirst, release of hormones, water balance

Thalamus
Controls: pain and pleasure sensations

Reticular Formation
Controls: messages going to the brain

Motor Centre
Controls: voluntary movements

The Cerebellum
The cerebellum, a folded structure smaller than the cerebrum, is located at the base of the brain. It is connected to the medulla oblongata, spinal cord and cerebrum by the pons.
Controls: balance and movement, muscle co-ordination, posture

The Medulla Oblongata
The medulla oblongata, located in the brain between the pons and the spinal cord, is involved in involuntary actions.
Controls: blood pressure, breathing, i.e. respiration, heartbeat

The Spinal Cord

The spinal cord extends from the medulla oblongata to the second lumbar vertebrae. It is enclosed in the protective spinal canal surrounded by the meninges and cerebrospinal fluid.

Cross-sections of the spinal cord show
- Inner grey matter, H-shaped in the centre, consisting of clusters of neuron cell bodies
- Outer white matter consisting of nerves travelling to and from the brain

REFLEXES

A reflex action is an automatic involuntary motor response to a sensory stimulus that does not involve a message being sent to the brain. An impulse travels along the reflex arc.

The stages involved in a reflex reaction are:
- Sensory receptors receive a stimulus
- An impulse passes along the sensory fibre
- Motor nerve fibre causes the muscle to contract
- Reaction or response occurs
- Separate impulse sent to brain to inform it about the response

THE PERIPHERAL NERVOUS SYSTEM

The peripheral nervous system:
- Consists of cranial and spinal nerves
- Transmits impulses to and from the central nervous system

CRANIAL NERVES

Twelve pairs travel from the brain stem to the head and neck. Some are involved in mainly sensory and some motor functions while others are mixed and are known as mixed nerves. Examples of cranial nerves are sensory nerves (auditory, optic, olfactory) and motor nerves (facial, vagus).

SPINAL NERVES

Thirty-one pairs of mixed nerves branch from the vertebrae in the spinal cord to all the muscles of the body. Examples of spinal nerves are neck, thoracic, femoral and sciatic nerves.

AUTONOMIC NERVOUS SYSTEM

The autonomic nervous system controls unconscious involuntary actions involved in some body systems. The actions of the autonomic nervous system are controlled by the hypothalamus. The autonomic nervous system consists of the:

- *Sympathetic nervous system:*
Stimulates responses to emergencies by increasing oxygen supplies and speeding up the conversion of glycogen to glucose for use by the muscles.

- *Parasympathetic nervous system:*
Slows down these responses and returns the body to normal functions.

REPRODUCTIVE SYSTEMS

FEMALE REPRODUCTIVE SYSTEM

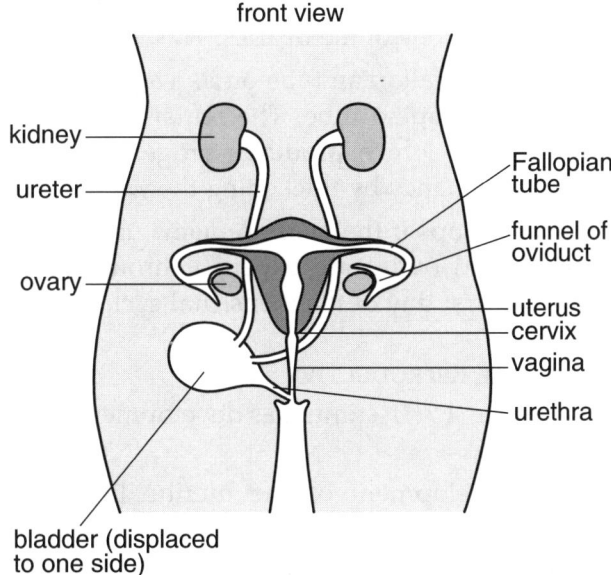

ORGANS OF THE FEMALE REPRODUCTIVE SYSTEM
The organs include the ovaries, fallopian tubes, the uterus or womb, cervix and vagina.

STRUCTURE
The oval-shaped ovaries are located on each side of the uterus, in the lower abdominal cavity. Ovaries contain a supply of unripe ova surrounded by a cluster of cells. These clusters of cells later form the Graafian follicle. Fallopian tubes link the ovaries to a muscular organ, the uterus or womb. The uterus narrows to form the neck or cervix which leads to the vagina.

Menstruation and Ovulation

Menstruation begins with puberty and continues until menopause around 40–55 years of age. The length of the menstrual cycle is on average about 28 days. It varies with individuals.

Ovulation occurs on the 14th day of the menstrual cycle. The menstrual flow lasts on average 5 days. The menstrual cycle consists of a series of changes that take place concurrently in the ovaries and the wall of the uterus, stimulated by hormones.

Ovulation and Menstruation

Every month one ovum develops and matures within the wall of a Graafian follicle. Graafian follicles produce oestrogen which stimulates the growth of the ovum and prepares the uterus for pregnancy. Each month an ovum is released from a Graafian follicle from one of the ovaries. This is called ovulation.

The ovum travels down the fallopian tube on its way to the uterus. An ovum may be fertilized in the fallopian tube. The remains of the Graafian follicle become the corpus luteum, which produces progesterone and continues to prepare the uterus for pregnancy by thickening the wall of the uterus.

Progesterone production stops if the ovum remains unfertilised. The lining of the uterus and unfertilised ovum are expelled through the vagina. This is called menstruation, the first day of the menstrual cycle.

Hormones in the Female Reproductive System

Follicle-stimulating hormone (FSH): stimulates development of the follicle, ovum and secretion of oestrogen.

Oestrogen: stimulates development of the uterine lining and inhibits the production of FSH.

Luteinising hormone (LH): Causes ovulation, the development of corpus luteum with the corpus luteum producing progesterone.

Progesterone: prepares the body by thickening the wall of the uterus, inhibits FSH and LH production. The drop in LH causes the corpus luteum to break down, progesterone levels fall, and the wall of the uterus breaks down resulting in menstruation.

Fertilisation

During sexual intercourse the tissues of the penis becomes distended with blood. The erect penis releases semen into the vagina of the female. Semen, containing millions of spermatozoa, swim through the cervix into the uterus, up the fallopian tubes, in search of an ovum. The sperm surround the ovum and only one sperm head is allowed to penetrate it. The sperm fuses with the ovum. This is the moment of fertilisation.

PREGNANCY

The fertilised egg divides to form new cells as it moves down the fallopian tubes into the uterus. It implants into the uterine wall, the endometrium. The new cell becomes a ball of cells from which develops the embryo and the embryonic membranes. Finger projections, villi, are attached to the uterine wall and absorb nutrients for the developing embryo. The placenta forms and filters oxygen, carbon dioxide, nutrients and waste products for the embryo.

At the 8-weeks stage, the developing embryo is called a foetus. The embryo is linked to the placenta by the umbilical cord and is protected from shocks by the amniotic sac. Increases in oestrogen and progesterone levels result in many changes in the body e.g. increases in size of uterus, breast size and body weight. Increased progesterone levels prevent miscarriage and inhibit menstruation. Pregnancy lasts about 40 weeks.

BIRTH

The head of the foetus lines up above the cervix in preparation for birth. The birth begins when oxytocin stimulates the contractions of the uterine muscles. The cervix becomes dilated and the amniotic membranes break, releasing the amniotic fluid. As the contractions become stronger the cervix widens and dilates fully to allow the baby's head though the cervix and vagina.

Once the baby is born, the umbilical cord is clamped at the naval. After birth the uterus contracts again to separate the placenta and the remaining umbilical cord. They are expelled from the body. This is called the afterbirth.

MALE REPRODUCTIVE SYSTEM

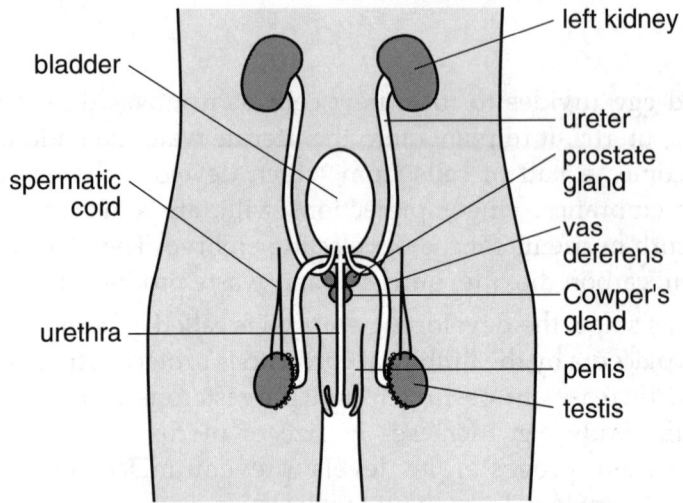

ORGANS OF THE MALE REPRODUCTIVE SYSTEM

The organs are the testes, epididymus, scrotum, penis, semi-vesicles, vas deferens, prostrate gland, Cowper's gland.

STRUCTURE

The testes are located in the scrotum outside the body. The testes consist of coiled seminiferous tubules that join together to form the epididymus. Sperm is produced within the tubules and released through the epididymus into vas deferens. The vas deferens is linked to the seminal vesicle and to the urethra by ducts.

The seminal vesicle, prostate gland and Cowper's gland secrete fluids which form semen to nourish the sperm. When the male is aroused the penis becomes erect. The sperm are released into the vas deferens and mix with the secreted fluids of the various glands and seminal vesicle. The sperm are activated by the secretion from the prostate gland. During sexual intercourse the semen is ejaculated from the penis into the female vagina.

HORMONES IN THE MALE REPRODUCTIVE SYSTEM

Follicle-stimulating hormone: stimulates the production of sperm.

Luteinising hormone: stimulates the production of testosterone.

THE RESPIRATORY SYSTEM

The respiratory system allows oxygen to be taken in from the air, transported to the cells and exchanged for carbon dioxide and water. Adults breathe about 15–20 times a minute. Exercise increases the demand for oxygen. The efficiency of the respiratory system is affected by smoking and diseases of the respiratory system.

STRUCTURE

The respiratory system consists of the passageways of the respiratory tract, two lungs, muscles involved in breathing (intercostal, abdominal) and the medulla oblongata.

SUMMARY OF THE RESPIRATORY TRACT

Nasal cavities and nose: warm and filter the inspired air by the cilia (hairs) so that impurities and dust cannot enter the passageways. Air becomes saturated with moisture.

Mouth: if air is breathed in through the mouth it is not filtered.

Pharynx: divides into two passages forming the oesophagus and the trachea. Air is warmed as in the nasal cavities.

Larynx: responsible for voice. Air passes through the vocal chords into the trachea. Air is humidified, filtered and warmed.

Epiglottis: prevents food 'going down the wrong way'.

Trachea: formed from C-shaped rings of cartilage, runs from the larynx, divides into the two bronchi at the base, lined with cilia and mucus membrane.

Bronchi: hoops of cartilage are present in the walls of the bronchi, they branch into thinner smaller tubes in each lung, the bronchioles.

Bronchioles: small branches without cartilage through which air passes on its way to clusters of air cells or sacs, the alveoli.

Alveoli: thin-walled structures with a spongy structure covered in a network of fine capillaries, through which the exchange or diffusion of gases occurs.

THE LUNGS

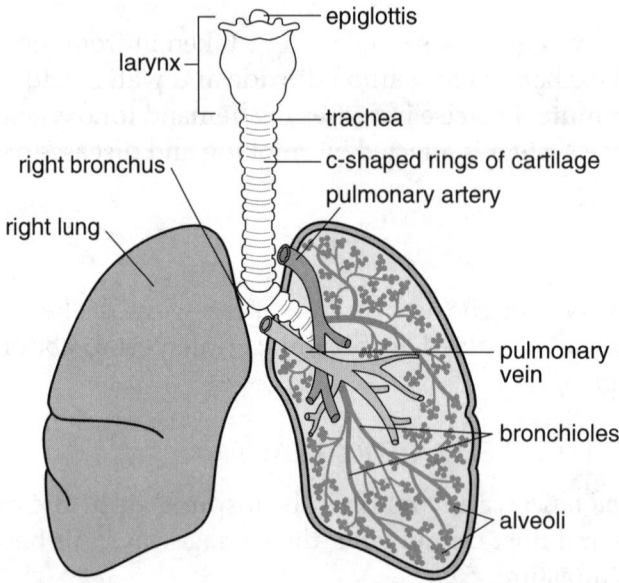

Position
The lungs are located in the chest or thoracic cavity, above the diaphragm. They are protected by the sternum, rib cage and intercostal muscles, with the heart in between them.

Shape
The lungs are conical in shape and are wider at the base than at the apex. The base of each lung rests on the diaphragm. The apex points upwards.

Structure of the Lungs
- Consist of purple spongy elastic tissue
- Surrounded by a protective membrane, the pleura
- Divided into lobes, the left lung into two lobes, the right lung into three lobes
- Consist of bronchi, bronchioles, alveoli, a network of blood vessels, nerves and lymphatics

The pulmonary arteries and veins, the main blood vessels of the lungs, and the bronchi are attached to the root of the lungs.

The Medulla Oblongata

The medulla oblongata controls the rate and depth of respiration. It is sensitive to levels of carbon dioxide in the body. Increased levels of carbon dioxide cause the medulla oblongata to respond by increasing the rate of breathing. The rate of breathing is slowed down when carbon dioxide levels are low during periods of inactivity.

Cycle of Respiration

- Inspiration
- Expiration
- Pause

The muscular movements involved in breathing are:
- Breathing in or inspiration
- Breathing out or expiration

Inspiration

During inspiration the diaphragm contracts, descends and flattens. The rib cage is raised by the contracting intercostal muscles. The volume of the thoracic cavity increases, pressure on the lungs is decreased and air is drawn into the lungs.

Expiration

During expiration the diaphragm relaxes and rises upwards. The rib cage falls as the intercostal muscles relax. The volume of the chest cavity is decreased, pressure on the lungs increases and air is expelled from the lungs.

Exchange of Gases or External Respiration

A diffusion of gases takes place between the alveoli and the surrounding network of blood capillaries. During inspiration, oxygen-rich air is drawn into the respiratory system until it reaches the alveoli. In the alveoli:
- Oxygen passes through the thin permeable wall of the alveoli into the capillaries where it is taken up by haemoglobin in the blood. Oxygen-rich blood is transported to the heart via the pulmonary veins and from there to all body cells.
- Carbon dioxide passes from the blood in the capillaries into the alveoli and is expelled from the lungs as stale air.

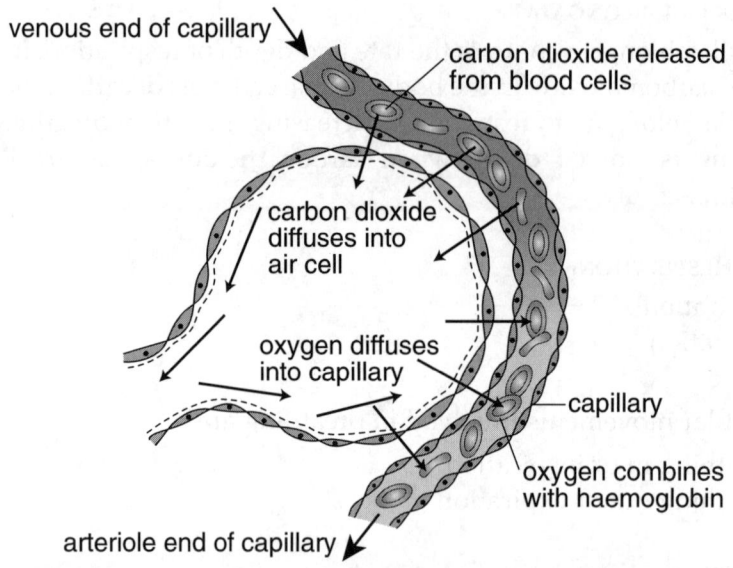

INTERNAL RESPIRATION OR CELLULAR RESPIRATION

This is the exchange of gases between the body cells and the blood. When the concentration of oxygen is high in the capillaries and low in the cells, the concentration of carbon dioxide is high in the cells and low in the capillaries. The gas in the area of high concentration moves to the area of low concentration. Oxygen diffuses through the capillary walls into the cells. Carbon dioxide diffuses through the cell walls into the capillaries. Energy is released.

EXAMPLES OF RESPIRATORY PROBLEMS AND DISEASES

The rate of breathing is affected by exercise, smoking and diseases of the respiratory system. Problems include bronchitis, colds, sore throats, emphysema, influenza, lung cancer, laryngitis, pleurisy, pneumonia, throat cancer and tuberculosis.

THE SKIN

The skin is one of the excretory organs of the body as well as a sensory organ. The skin consists of two layers, the epidermis and the dermis. It varies in thickness and covers the body.

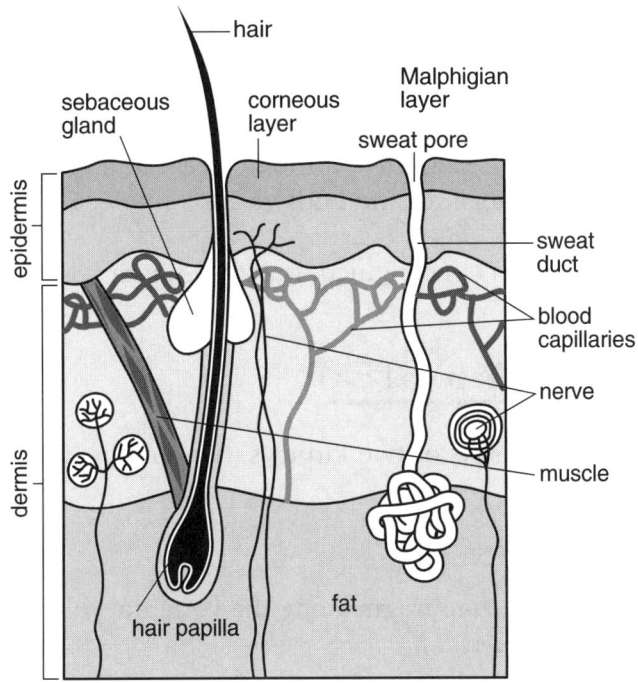

STRUCTURE

EPIDERMIS OR THE CORNEOUS LAYER

The epidermis, the outer layer of the skin, is composed of flattened dead cells which act as a protective layer. It does not have nerves or blood vessels. The outer layer is constantly wearing away and being replaced by cells from underneath. Below the dead cells, lie layers of living cells, including the malphigian layer, containing the pigment melanin.

THE DERMIS

The dermis, a thick layer lying under the epidermis, is composed of connective tissue. The dermis contains:

Hair follicles: epidermal cells which produce new hair cells
Sebaceous glands: produce sebum to lubricate hair and skin
Sweat glands: excrete sweat (salt, water, urea), regulate body temperature
Nerve endings: stimulate responses to sensations e.g. cold, heat
Blood vessels: transport nutrients and oxygen to cells
Erector muscles: insulating reaction, regulate body temperature
Adipose tissue: insulates body, acts as an energy store

GENERAL FUNCTIONS OF THE SKIN

- Protects against ultra-violet rays, injury, infections, bacteria, chemicals
- Regulates body temperature by evaporation of sweat
- Acts as an insulator
- Removes waste e.g. salt, urea, through sweat ducts and pores
- Prevents loss of moisture and body fluids
- Responds to sensations
- Produces vitamin D in conjunction with sunlight

THE URINARY SYSTEM

The urinary system consists of two kidneys, two ureters, urinary bladder and urethra.

POSITION OF THE KIDNEYS

- Lie just under the diaphragm along the vertebral column towards the back of the abdomen
- Surrounded by a protective layer of fat

SHAPE, COLOUR AND SIZE

Bean-shaped organs, dark red in colour, about 12 cm long.

BASIC STRUCTURE OF A KIDNEY

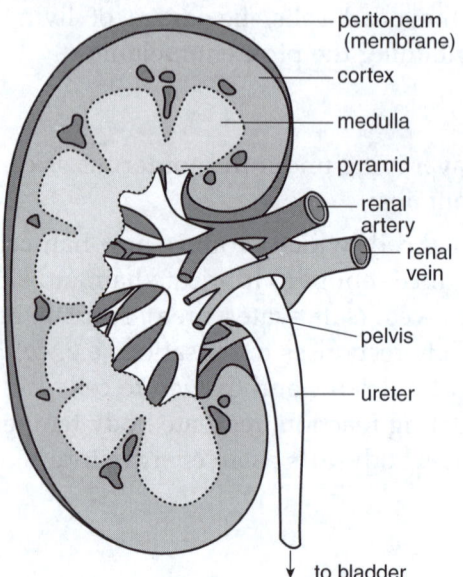

Each kidney has three main areas. These are:
- The outer fibrous capsule or peritoneum
- The cortex or the middle darker layer
- The medulla or the inner layer containing the 'pyramids'

Blood enters the hilum of the kidney through the renal artery. Blood leaves the kidney via the renal vein. Urine is collected in the pelvis of the kidney and leaves through the ureter, is stored in the bladder, and removed from the body through the urethra.

THE NEPHRONS: POINTS TO NOTE

Kidneys are composed of a mass of tubules called nephrons. They are responsible for the formation of urine. Each nephron consists of a network of capillaries, the glomerulus, located in the cortex and a renal tubule. The glomerulus is surrounded by a cup-shaped membrane called Bowman's capsule. Fluid is filtered from the glomerulus through Bowman's capsule into the proximal tubule, the loop of Henle and the distal convoluted tubule. The distal tubule empties its contents into a collecting duct which passes into the pelvis of the kidney.

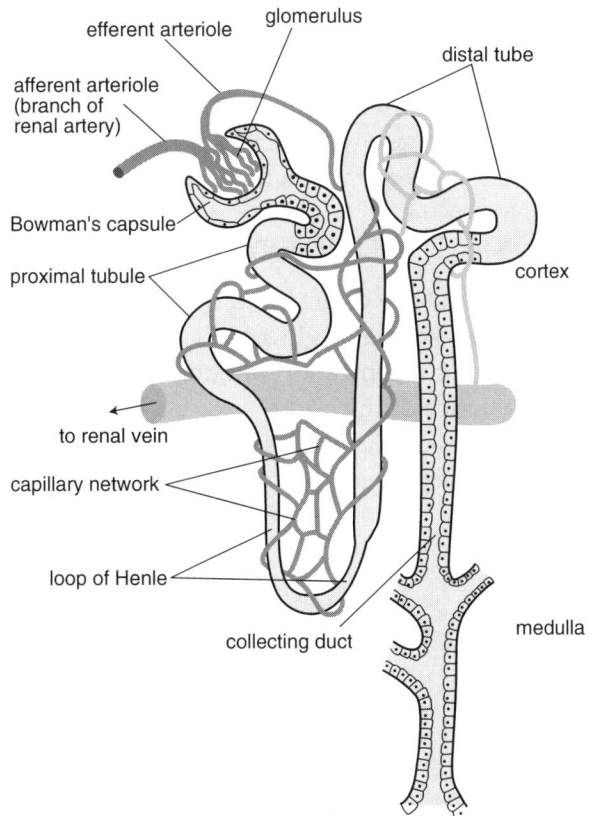

THE RENAL CIRCULATION

- After entering the kidney, the renal artery divides into smaller arteries and arterioles. All blood is filtered through the glomerulus and Bowman's capsule. The afferent arteriole enters Bowman's capsule then subdivides into capillaries and forms the glomerulus.
- The blood vessel leading away from the glomerulus is the efferent arteriole. It breaks up into another network of capillaries and surrounds the proximal tubule and the loop of Henle.
- Useful substances are re-absorbed from the filtrate, assisted by the villi of the proximal tubule (selective absorption). Further re-absorption takes place in the loop of Henle and the distal tubule. The resulting filtrate becomes urine.

Urine passes into the collecting duct for transport to the ureter, the bladder and the urethra, from where it passes out of the body when the sphincter muscle relaxes. Capillaries, with deoxygenated blood, unite to form veins and drain into the renal vein. Filtered deoxygenated blood returns to the heart via the renal veins and superior venae cavae.

OSMOREGULATION

This is the process controlling the amounts of water and sodium in the body. The pituitary hormone called the anti-diuretic hormone (ADH) is involved in this process. ADH levels increase when urine concentration increases e.g. due to diarrhoea. ADH levels decrease when the blood becomes too dilute.

GENERAL FUNCTIONS OF THE KIDNEYS

- Filter nitrogenous wastes e.g. urea and other toxins from the blood
- Control loss of water, salts and glucose
- Control and regulate concentration of body fluids
- Regulate water balance of the body
- Regulate pH of the blood (*homeostasis*)
- Regulate urinary losses (*osmoregulation*)

PART II A
A PLACE TO LIVE

9

HOUSING

FACTORS INFLUENCING CHOICE OF HOME

- Location, community, environment
- Money available, cost of homes on market
- Buying or renting or sharing with others
- Type of home, size, low maintenance, security, garden
- Ease of access to services e.g. transport, facilities
- Family size, couple with or without children
- Suitability for people with special needs
- Proximity to work, family, friends
- Potential resale value

CLASSIFICATION OF HOUSING

Housing can be grouped into apartments or flats, bedsits, houses (terraced, semi-detached, detached), bungalows, maisonettes and mobile home.

TYPES OF OWNERSHIP

OWNER-OCCUPIER

- The legal owner
- Freehold (no ground rent) or leasehold (pay ground rent)
- Mortgaged, title deeds remain with the mortgagor (bank, building society)

LOCAL AUTHORITY TENANT
- Home and land belongs to the Local Authority
- Points system used to allocate homes
- Rents are based on the ability to pay

RENTED HOMES
- Home owned by an individual, a family or company
- Rent charged is based on demand for location
- Rents can vary and increase according to market trends
- Variety available e.g. apartment, bedsit, house
- Limited tenant rights
- Can be located in a tax designated area

RENTING A HOME

CHOICES
- Private rented sector (individuals, companies)
- Social housing sector (Local Authority)

POINTS TO CONSIDER: SIMILAR TO BUYING A HOME
When renting consider:
- Type of lease
- Money available
- Location and facilities
- Size of household (couple, children, grandparents)
- Type of home
- Energy efficiency, insulation, heating, etc.
- Interior of house, storage, decoration
- Natural environment, garden, local parks

LEGISLATION: PRIVATE RENTED SECTOR HOUSING
- Housing (Registration of Rented Houses) Regulations 1996: houses to be registered with the local authority
- Housing (Rent Books) Regulations 1993: entitles tenants to a rent book with records of monies paid
- Housing (Standards for Rented Houses) Regulations 1993: dealing with the physical standards of rented accommodation
- Housing (Miscellaneous Provisions) Act 1992: section dealing with security of tenure
- Housing (Private Rented Dwellings) Act 1982: dealing with controlled dwellings

Advantages of Renting
- More affordable than buying
- Can move more easily in the future
- Landlord responsible for structural repairs
- Landlord responsible for maintenance of services
- Must comply with legislations outlined
- Deposit returned at the end of the stay
- Possibility of sharing, to reduce costs

Disadvantages of Renting
- Not an investment for the future
- Limited space if house has been divided up
- Could be noisy with other tenants close by
- Undesirable interior decoration/design
- No garden or outside storage area
- Sharing might not work out

Summary of Costs Involved in Renting
- Solicitor, checking of lease
- Property Agency fee
- Deposit (returned)
- Insurance of contents
- Regular rent payments
- Household bills
- Furniture if partially furnished
- Maintenance fees in some instances

LOCAL AUTHORITY HOUSING

Acquiring a Local Authority House
The procedure involved is:
- Fill out an application form
- Application is assessed by the local authority
- Name is put on local authority waiting list if accepted
- Houses are allocated in order of priority
- Rent is determined by individual's income
- Rent increases if income increases
- Differential rent system is applied

Rented Local Authority Housing
All local authorities have a selection of accommodation in rural and urban locations. A points system operates. There is reasonable security of tenure.

Extra Options when on Housing List
Individuals can avail of Shared Ownership Scheme or Tenant Purchase Scheme.

Other Possibilities
Individuals may qualify for Local Authority loans and low cost housing sites.

BUYING A HOME
In Ireland:
- 80% approx. of people own their own home
- Includes houses being bought privately and from Local Authorities
- Most people take out a mortgage to buy their home

Factors Influencing Buyer
- Money available, savings and borrowings
- Sources of finance
- Location, proximity to services and work
- Size of household
- Individual requirements e.g. special needs
- Type of home required/available
- Present structure, does it need work?
- Energy efficiency, insulation, heating, etc.
- Future upkeep (easy maintenance)
- Interior of house, space and location of rooms and services
- Natural environment, garden, local parks

Advantages to Buyer
- A good investment
- An asset for the future
- Security
- Mortgage tax relief

Disadvantages to Buyer
- Expensive initially
- Organising deposit, mortgage and legal work
- Time involved

- Long-term financial planning necessary
- Will have to make sacrifices
- Repayments not made could result in repossession
- Commuting distance to work
- Affordable housing not available close to work

SUMMARY OF COSTS INVOLVED
Initial Costs include:
- Deposit, solicitor's fees/legal fees, stamp duty
- Lending agency fees, application fee, searches, survey
- Mortgage legal costs
- Buyer's survey

On-going Costs include:
Monthly re-payments, household insurance, local charges, maintenance, repairs and, possibly, ground rent.

SOURCES OF FINANCE FOR MORTGAGES
- Assurance companies
- Banks
- Building societies
- Local Authorities
- Family, friends

STEPS INVOLVED IN BUYING A HOUSE
Contact the lending agency to check out:
- How much can you borrow?
- What conditions apply e.g. credit rating, savings?
- Information required by the lending institution?
- Other conditions of the lending agency?
- Loan period?
- How to apply for a mortgage?
- What forms need to be completed?
- Home Bond?
- Floor Area Certificate?
- Available grants?

Then:
- Hire a solicitor
- View a range of properties within your budget
- Choose a house
- Get surveyor to check it out
- Visit Local Authority Planning Office, check development plans
- Apply for mortgage
- Pay deposit on signing the contract in the presence of the required legal people
- Buyer's solicitor and lending agency will check title documents
- Transaction is completed when buyer's solicitor is satisfied that all is legally correct
- Remainder of purchase price handed over

OTHER WAYS OF ACQUIRING A HOME

Consider Housing Co-operatives, Voluntary Housing, purchasing from the Local Authority, building your own or living with parents.

DESIRABLE AMENITIES IN NEW HOUSING DEVELOPMENTS

- Low density housing, detached if possible
- Housing arranged around small cul-de-sacs
- Near shops, library, schools, bus/train route
- Landscaped green areas and open spaces
- Finished footpaths and roads
- Adequate public lighting

BUILDING A HOME

People who may be involved: Auctioneer, Architect, Builder, Structural Engineers, Solicitors, Surveyors, Local Authority, Planning Office, Interior Designer, Landscape Gardener.

Factors to Consider when Buying A Site

The characteristics of a good site are:
- Slightly sloping, bright and sunny site with a pleasant view
- Well drained with no areas of dampness
- Free of flooding from rivers, drains and artesian pools
- Secure, not too isolated, near a road
- Close to water and sewage systems if possible

- Suitable for septic tank and water well
- Cleared of overgrown bushes
- Free of trees close to the planned position of the house
- Not reclaimed land or too close to a river

BUILDING REGULATIONS

Regulations govern specific aspects of building a house e.g. position of house on site, drainage, fire safety, foundations, materials used, services (water, sewage) systems (insulation, heating, lighting, ventilation), weather resistance. Enforcement of the building regulations standards ensures that a new home will be a safe and healthy place.

PLANNING PERMISSION

Planning permission is necessary for alterations to existing homes (greater than 23 sq.m.), change of use of a home e.g. business purposes, conversions e.g. garages, and for building new homes. Porches to the front or back of a home, conservatories, domestic extensions to the back of the house under 23 sq.m., satellite and TV aerials are generally exempt. Check the latest rules and regulations, as over time, they can change.

Types of Planning Permission

Outline Planning Permission; Planning Approval; Full Planning Permission

SUMMARY OF PLANNING PERMISSION PROCESS

- Applicant publishes notice of application in national or local paper
- Notice erected on site following specific guidelines
- Lodge application, plus fee, with local authority planning office
- Application is put on the planning register for public to view
- Written submissions or objections against the proposed plans may be lodged
- Local authority official inspects proposed site
- Planning authority considers planning application
- After about 3 months, outline planning permission, approval or full planning permission may be granted.

Those who object are notified of the final decision in writing by the Local Authority.

CONSTRUCTION OF A HOME

TYPES OF FOUNDATIONS
Pile (sunken pillars); Raft (flat layer); Strip (under perimeter wall)

TYPES OF FLOORS
Solid (concrete); Suspended (wooden joists, tongued and grooved)

DAMP PROOF COURSE
Building regulations demand that builders include damp proof membrane to ensure damp will not rise up through floors and walls. Materials used are felt, plastic and polythene.

WALLS
Exterior walls
- Are load-bearing walls
- Are cavity walls
- Support roof and upper floors, including attic
- Have a variety of finishes e.g. brick, decorative stone

Interior walls
- Form room partition walls
- Consist of wooden frame and plasterboard or block walls

DOORS AND WINDOWS
- Aluminium, PVC or wood
- Double or single glazing
- Safety glass in external or internal doors
- Variety of colours, shapes and sizes

INSULATION
Houses must be insulated, following the building regulations, to prevent or slow down heat loss through doors, floors, roofs, walls and windows.

Areas	Materials and Methods
Doors	Draught excluders; foam, metal, rubber strips Door curtains Draught excluders on letter box

Areas	Materials and Methods
Floors	Fill cracks between floor boards
	Foil
	Underlay and carpet
	Underlay and vinyl flooring
Roofs	Attic insulation e.g. fibre glass
	Loose polystyrene pellets (do not insulate under water storage tank)
Walls	Foam-filled cavity walls
	Insulated plasterboard
	Polystyrene sheeting
Windows	Blinds and lined curtains
	Draught excluders, foam or rubber
	Double glazing
	Thermal lining on curtains
Water cylinders	Lagging jacket
Water pipes	Foam stripping or split foam tubes

10

SERVICES

WATER AND SANITATION

Building regulations and by-laws, enforced by the local authority, ensure a fresh water supply free from contamination to all homes. Proposed drainage, water and sewage systems for new homes are checked by the local authority planning office. Major alterations to drainage systems in any home require planning permission.

WATER

Urban and Rural Water Supplies

Location	Sources
Cities and Towns	Local Authority Water Supply
Rural Areas	Deep Wells and Rural Water Supply

Water Supply for Rural Homes

Wells provide water for rural homes. For safety reasons, all wells should be securely covered.

Rainwater collects on non-porous layers of rock to form springs or when the rock is bored, it forms a well.

A lining of concrete or steel is used to prevent contaminants seeping into the well from the surrounding land. Following drilling and lining, a pump is fitted to bring water to the surface and into the home. Filters and water softeners may be fitted.

Types of Well
- Deep wells
- Shallow wells

Water Supply for Cities and Towns

Natural or man-made lakes, positioned on high ground, are used as reservoirs to store water for towns and cities.

Treatments Involved

Process	What happens
Filtration	Impurities are suspended on filterbeds of sand and gravel
Sedimentation	Remaining impurities settle to the bottom as water flows into storage reservoirs
Chlorination	To sterilise the water, controlled quantities of chlorine are added
Fluoridation	Fluorine is added to strengthen teeth and improve dental health
Softening	Chlorine of lime added to hard water in reservoirs

Water hardness

Calcium or magnesium bicarbonates, or calcium or magnesium sulphates, cause hardness in water. These are absorbed from the surrounding rocks and soil.

Problems Created by Hard Water
- Hair becomes dull, skin becomes dry
- Soap does not lather, detergents do not form suds
- Scum forms, clings to baths, clothes, sinks, skin, and hair
- 'Furring up' of central heating pipes and kettles
- Water system and kettles become less efficient

Softening Hard Water
Water can be softened by:
- Adding chlorine of lime during water treatment
- Adding washing soda when washing clothes
- Adding bath salts to bath water
- Boiling water at home in small amounts
- Using a commercial water softener

Household Water Supply
- Water from reservoir is brought to the main pipes
- Mains bring water to the service pipe at the house
- Stopcock outside the house controls the supply (on/off)
- A service pipe enters the house near the kitchen sink
- Connecting pipe brings water to the cold tap
- A pipe brings water to the storage cistern or attic tank
- Storage tank is made of galvanised iron or plastic
- A ball valve controls water levels or rate of fill
- An overflow pipe takes away excess water in emergencies

The water in the attic storage tank is not drinking water. The storage tank should be covered and insulated. Do not insulate under the storage tank. Water pipes should be lagged.

Type of Hot Water Systems
- Direct System
- Indirect System

The Direct System
- Cold water from storage cylinder supplies the boiler
- Water is heated in the boiler, rises to top and travels through pipes to the storage cylinder
- Taps in kitchen and bathrooms draw off the heated water
- Cold water from the attic storage tank is piped into storage cylinder to replace it
- Cold water is supplied to the boiler (gas, oil or solid fuel) for heating

The Indirect System
The indirect system is linked to the central heating system. Two circulations of water take place. Both systems are separate and self-contained. Expansion pipes from both systems carry steam to an expansion tank in the attic.

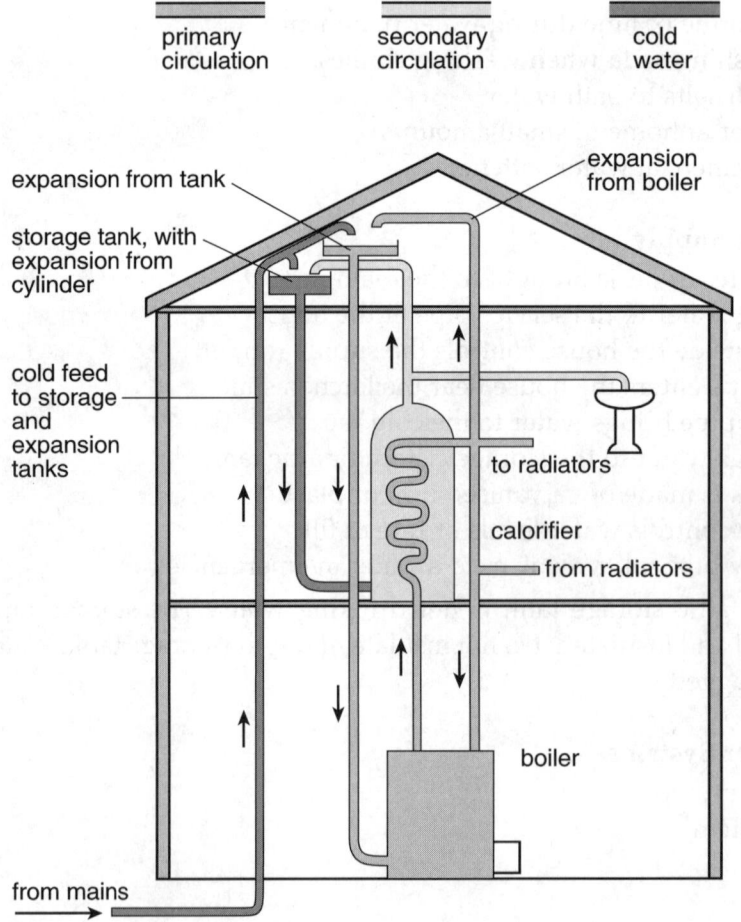

The Primary Circulation
- Water is heated in central heating boiler for radiators
- Heated water rises from the boiler, passes through a heat exchanger and indirectly heats the water in the storage cylinder
- The heated water passes from the heat exchanger to radiators
- Cooled water returns for heating in the boiler

Secondary Circulation
- Cold water from the attic storage tank is piped to the storage cylinder
- Heat exchanger heats this cold water
- Hot water is drawn off for use in bathroom and kitchen
- Cold water, from the attic storage tank, replaces hot water in the storage cylinder

Immersion Heaters
Immersion heaters are fitted with single or dual enclosed electric elements. A single element heats sufficient water for a sink and a dual element heats sufficient water for a bath. Water is heated thermostatically within the cylinder. Hot water is available all year.

SANITATION

Waste Disposal
- Waste can be in dry or wet forms
- Recycling is recommended
- Use collection banks for cloths, glass, metal, paper and oil
- Deliver clothes in good condition to charity shops
- Remake clothes into garments for children or use fabrics in craftwork
- Set up a compost heap in the garden

Local authorities or private refuse collectors collect household waste once a week. There is a charge for this in many areas.

Types of waste	Examples
Inorganic	Cans, cardboard, delph, fibre, glass, plastic, metal, newspapers
Organic	Left-over food, plants, vegetable peelings Sewage Waste from baths and sinks

Rural Areas

When a refuse collection service is not available:
- Use collection banks for a variety of inorganic items
- Set up a compost heap well away from the house
- Dig a refuse pit for organic materials

When not linked into a urban sewage system:
- Install a septic tank away from the house with waste from baths, sinks and toilets piped into it
- Clean out septic tanks occasionally

Septic Tanks

Domestic effluent is stored in a large tank, decomposes into harmless substances due to the action of bacteria and gradually seeps through a series of pipes into the surrounding ground.

Cleaning Drains

Agents used to clean drains around the house include bleaches, disinfectants, commercial drain cleaners and washing soda. Because of pollution it is essential to check that the cleaning agent used is environmentally friendly.

A Sewage Treatment Plant

- Domestic waste (baths, showers and sinks) empties into the main drain gulley
- Separate pipes, with ventilated tops, bring waste from toilets to the main drain
- Domestic waste and sewage, is brought to the sewage treatment plant
- Sewage is filtered, breaks up and solids settle to bottom of the sewage tanks
- Bacteria work on the sewage, breaking it into harmless compounds
- End products are released into rivers or sea or used for fertilisers

Effects of Poor Drainage and Waste Disposal

- Contaminated water supply
- Bad smells outside or inside the house
- Increase in flies and rats
- Illness e.g. cholera, dysentery, gastro-enteritis

WASTE DISPOSAL IN KITCHENS

Small easy to clean plastic or metal bins may be used in kitchens, emptied and disinfected daily. Some kitchens have a waste disposal unit fitted as part of the sink unit. This machine grinds and chops up kitchen waste. The residue is washed into the drain by a continuous flow of water. Waste disposal units are convenient and hygienic and reduce the amount of waste in the kitchen bin.

HOME HEATING

FUELS

Fuels used in home heating are:
- Electricity
- Gas (bottled, tanks and mains)
- Oil
- Solid fuel

TRANSFER OF HEAT

Heat is transferred by:
- Conduction
- Convection
- Radiation

HEATING SYSTEMS AVAILABLE

Systems	Examples
Portable room heater	Bottled gas heater
	Convector heater
	Electric heater
	Fan heater
	Oil-filled radiator
Fixed heating appliances	Electric coal-effect fire
	Gas coal-effect fire
	Solid fuel fire (enclosed)
	Storage heater
	Wall-mounted heater
Central heating systems	Electric underfloor heating
	Small bore wet system
	Storage heating

PLANNING A HOME HEATING SYSTEM

When planning a heating system consider:
- Requirements of the household
- Choices available, design and safety of systems
- Budget available, installation and running costs
- Energy efficiency of system
- Potential pollution problems
- Regulations regarding the use of fuels e.g. coal
- Special offers e.g. Gas Company, ESB schemes
- Storage of fuels, space, deliveries
- Safety

ADVANTAGES OF FIXED ROOM HEATERS

- Easy to clean and maintain
- Safer than portable models
- Sturdy and long lasting

DISADVANTAGES OF FIXED ROOM HEATERS

- Cannot be moved around to heat up cold areas of a room
- Expensive
- Open fires and solid fuel room heaters need cleaning
- Some models take longer to heat up than portable varieties

ADVANTAGES OF PORTABLE ROOM HEATERS

- Variety of options and designs
- Used to introduce heat when needed
- Convenient, easy to move around
- Heat up very quickly and efficiently

DISADVANTAGE OF PORTABLE ROOM HEATERS

- Not safe if there are toddlers around
- Some models are easy to overturn
- Loose flexes could cause someone to fall
- Should not be moved when lit e.g. oil, gas
- Dry out air in room

CENTRAL HEATING

TYPES OF CENTRAL HEATING SYSTEMS
Background Heating
- General heating, provides a little heat
- Needs to be supplemented by other systems

Partial Central Heating
- Section of the house heated
- Heat provided by a back boiler or a solid fuel cooker
- Needs to be supplemented by other systems

Full Central Heating
- Fully automatic, provides a range of temperatures
- Heats the entire house

SMALL BORE WET SYSTEM
This system combines central heating and the heating of domestic hot water.

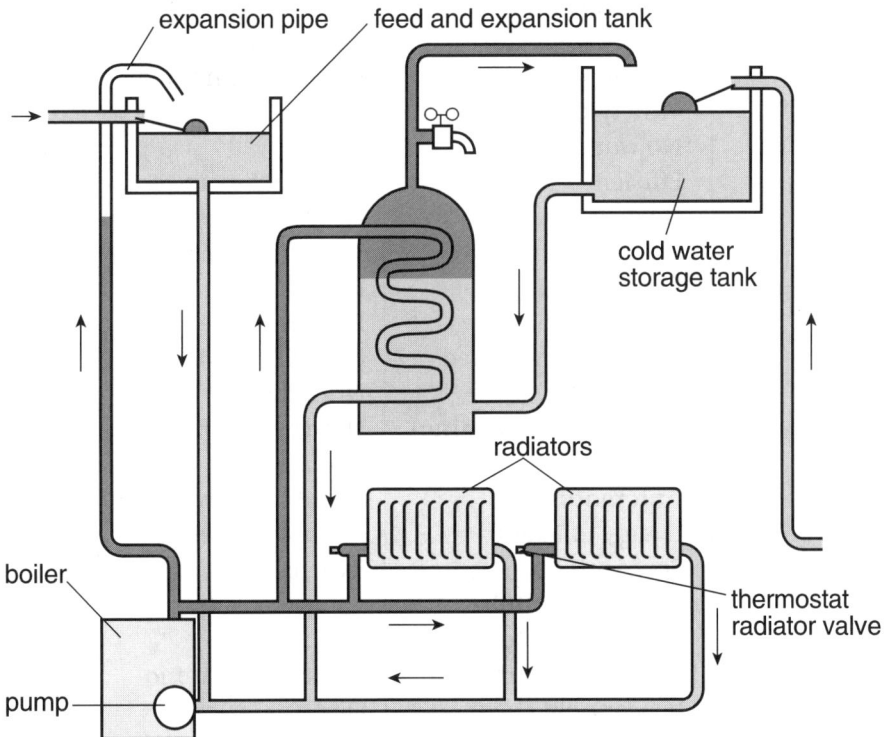

Primary Circulation: Heating the Radiators
- Thermostats control the water temperature
- Timers control the on/off of the system
- Central heating boiler heats cold water
- Heated water is pumped through the heat exchanger and passes through small bore pipes to the radiators
- Cooled water from radiators returns to boiler for heating
- Cycle of heating begins again
- Steam from boiler escapes into attic feed and expansion tank

SECONDARY CIRCULATION: HEATING WATER
Water from the attic water tanks enters the bottom of the storage cylinder. Water in the storage cylinder (hot press) is indirectly heated by the water in the enclosed heat exchanger. The two systems are entirely separate and never mix. Hot water is drawn off from the top of the storage cylinder by taps around the house. Cold water replaces the hot water at the bottom of the cylinder.

Fuels	Advantages	Disadvantages
Electricity	Available on demand Clean, efficient Easy to use Variety of appliances No waste	Dries air in room Expensive Power cuts, no heat
Bottled gas	Efficient Heats up quickly	Unattractive in room Cylinders very heavy Ventilation needed
Natural gas	Easy to use Efficient, no waste No storage required Versatile (cooking and heating)	Expensive Fitter must be qualified Possibility of leaks Dries air Needs ventilation
Oil	Easy to use Automatic Energy efficient Economical Easy to maintain Easy to store fuel	Storage tank Portables - fire risk Portables smell Expensive
Solid fuel	Pleasant in a room Reasonably cheap Helps ventilation Can provide hot water Creates atmosphere	Constant cleaning Dirty Bulky storage Not efficient Pollutes environment

THERMOSTATS

Thermostats are devices that control temperature levels. Thermostats are used in heating systems, heating appliances and household appliances e.g. cookers, irons. All thermostats work on the principle of a bimetallic strip. This strip consists of two metals, bonded together, which expand at different rates when heated. The strip is heated as the electricity flows through it and on heating it bends away from the contact point. The electric circuit is broken. As the strip cools contact is made again. Electricity flows and the appliance heats up again.

ELECTRICITY IN THE HOME

TERMINOLOGY

Amperes: rate of flow of the electric current

Good conductors: do not resist the flow of electricity

Poor conductors: offer great resistance to electricity

Electric current: the flow of electrons or electricity

Kilowatt-hour: measurement of a unit of electrical consumption

Voltage: the pressure driving electric current through the wire

Watts: measurement of rate at which different appliances use electricity.

1000 Watts per hour = one unit of electricity

HOUSEHOLD ELECTRICITY SUPPLY

- ESB service cable provides the home with electricity
- Service cable connects to a sealed ESB fuse box in the home
- From the sealed fuse box electricity flows through the meter
- Meters record the amount of electricity used
- Meters are located in sealed external boxes for meter readings
- From the meter, electricity flows to the consumer unit, located indoors
- Consumer unit contains mains switch, fuse box, miniature circuit breakers, residual current devices
- Current is supplied to the various power points and lights around the house

TYPES OF ELECTRICAL CIRCUITS

Radial circuits: used for large appliances e.g. cookers, immersion heaters. Each appliance has its own fuse

Ring circuits: a number of sockets are attached to a continuous wire passing around the house forming a ring circuit

ELECTRICITY AND SAFETY

- Do not mix electricity and water
- Never overload circuit
- Buy electrical appliances with recognised safety symbols
- Avoid overuse of adaptors and extension cables
- Ensure equipment is always in perfect condition
- Replace damaged equipment, flexes, plugs, sockets and switches
- Do not use portable electrical heaters or radios in bathrooms
- Use the recommended lights and shaver sockets in bathrooms
- Use pull cords for wall-mounted heaters and shavers
- Unplug equipment before cleaning
- Unplug all appliances at night before going to bed
- Never fill a kettle without unplugging
- Avoid trailing flexes
- Never dry clothes near or on electric fires

Double Insulation Mark: appliances carrying the double insulation mark have two-core flex without an earth wire and are doubly insulated.

ELECTRICITY AND ECONOMY

ALL-ELECTRIC GOLD SHIELD HOMES

Homes are designed to be energy efficient with reduced running costs. Insulation, central heating and water heater systems are designed to fit in with this concept. Nightsaver electricity is used in these homes.

NIGHTSAVER ELECTRICITY

Low-cost electricity, provided at night, reduces the cost of standard units by 60%. Large domestic appliances can be operated using this system e.g. dishwashers, driers and washing machines. The cost of appliances that run continuously e.g. freezers is also reduced. Storage heaters make use of low-cost night-time electricity and heat is released during the day.

ELECTRICITY AND SAFETY FEATURES

Safety features in modern electrical systems are:
- Double insulation on appliances
- Earthing and fuses
- Miniature circuit breakers
- Residual current devices
- Shuttered sockets

LIGHTING IN THE HOME

REASONS FOR GOOD LIGHTING

Good Lighting is essential to:
- See what we are doing
- See in the home at night
- Prevent accidents
- Prevent eye problems, for visual comfort
- Create atmosphere within a room

FACTORS INFLUENCING LIGHTING REQUIREMENTS

- Amount of natural light in a room
- Type of work or activity
- Use of room e.g. kitchen, study, living room
- Dark and shady areas
- Atmosphere to be created
- Safety requirements e.g. stairs, steps
- Types of lighting systems available, fitments, etc.
- Appearance of fitments and cleaning required

PROPERTIES OF LIGHT

Light rays can be absorbed, diffused, dispersed, reflected or refracted.

TYPES, EXAMPLES AND SOURCES OF LIGHTING

ARTIFICIAL
- Filament: bulbs
- Fluorescent: bulbs, strip
- Compact Fluorescent Lamps (CFLs): bulbs

NATURAL
- Sunlight: doors, windows, glass bricks

Artificial Lighting
Artificial lighting is efficient, decorative or functional and safe.

Filament Lighting
Filament bulbs consist of thin curled tungsten filaments supported by wires within a clear or opal glass bulb. Argon gas fills the bulb and prevents the tungsten filament from vaporising as it becomes white hot when the bulb is switched on. Bulb wattage: 25w, 40w, 60w, 75w, 150w, 200w.

Fluorescent Lighting
A glass tube, consisting of an inner coating of phosphor, lights up when the electrodes at each end cause vaporisation of the mercury present when the light is turned on. The phosphor absorbs the ultraviolet light produced by the mercury. Wattage increases with the length of the fluorescent tubes which vary from 30 cm to 2.5 m. Fluorescent tubes are available in straight, circular or curved shapes.

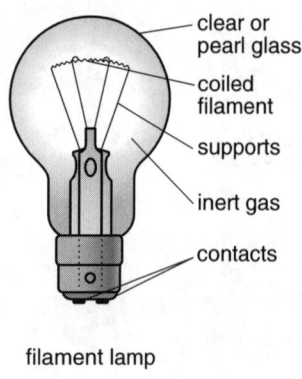

filament lamp

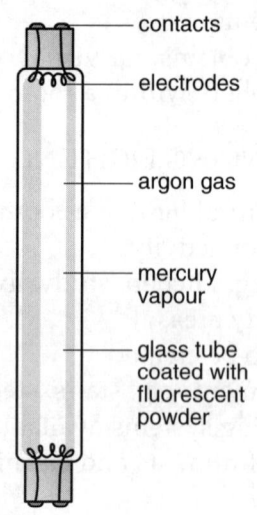

fluorescent lamp

Compact Fluorescent Lights
These are energy-efficient bulbs which last 8 times longer and use 80% less electricity than filament bulbs.

Types of Lighting
Accent: used to light up displays or an area in a room
Direct: for specific tasks e.g. reading, board games
General: for even background lighting in a room

PLANNING A LIGHTING SYSTEM

Factors to consider include:
- Function of room
- Safety issues, employ a qualified electrician
- Quality fitments, cost involved
- Desired lighting effect (day and evening)
- Position of wiring, switches, socket, fitments
- Easy to clean attractive systems

LIGHTING ARRANGEMENTS

Room	Lighting
Bathroom	Good general background lighting
	Central diffused or fluorescent fitting
	Light with pull cord near bathroom mirror
Bedroom	Good general background lighting
	Central diffused fitting
	Bedside lamps
	Strip-light at dressing table
Children's rooms	Good general background lighting
	Central diffused fitting with dimmer switch
	Bedside lamp, out of reach with safety switch
	Desk/study lamp for older children
Dining room	Good general background lighting
	Central light, rise and fall fitting
	Table lamps or wall lights
	Dimmer switches for softer lighting
Hall, stairs/landing	Good quality general lighting
	Lights in hall, over the stairs, on landing
	Steps should be well light
	Use two way switches
	Table lamps in hall
	Be safety conscious at all times
Kitchen	General background lighting
	Central fluorescent light
	Strip lighting over working surfaces
	Strip lighting over cooker hob
Living room	General background lighting
	Table lamps around the room
	Specific lamps for activities, e.g., reading
	Accent lighting for photographs, paintings
	Wall fittings with dimmers for atmosphere

VENTILATION IN THE HOME

PURPOSES OF VENTILATION

- Provides a supply of fresh air
- Prevents condensation especially in kitchens and bathrooms
- Removes stale air with impurities
- Removes cooking smells and other odours

CHARACTERISTICS OF GOOD VENTILATION

- Air is replaced at least once every hour
- Temperature should not drop too much
- Draughts should not result

Fresh Air Contains:	Stale Air Contains:
20.96% oxygen	16.96% oxygen
79.00% nitrogen	79% nitrogen (same as in fresh air)
0.04% carbon dioxide	4.04% carbon dioxide (increased in stale air)

Problems Associated with Inadequate Ventilation
- Risk of infections e.g. respiratory, colds
- Lower levels of concentration
- Feeling tired and drowsy, getting headaches
- Increased humidity and condensation levels
- Damage to walls, paintwork and wallpaper

CONDENSATION

Water vapour turns into water droplets and drips down mirrors, walls, windows and all shiny cold, non-absorbent surfaces. *Causes of condensation*: large amounts of steam in bathrooms and kitchens with poor ventilation and plenty of smooth cold surfaces.

HUMIDITY

Humidity is the amount of water vapour contained in air: low levels in cold air, higher levels in warmer air. Low humidity ranges from 20 to 50% moisture, high humidity is >90%.

Problems Associated with Condensation
- Chest problems (respiratory system)
- Damaged paintwork, wallpaper, wooden surfaces
- Damaged metal equipment, rusting
- Dangerously slippy floors
- Mould on ceilings, clothes, walls, wood

Prevention of Condensation
- Avoid overuse of cold shiny smooth surfaces e.g. tiles
- Choose soft furnishings to balance the smooth surfaces
- Control moisture content of the air, good ventilation
- Improve system of insulation, increase room temperatures

THE METHODS OF VENTILATION

Artificial	Air conditioning
	Cooker hoods
	Extractor fans
Natural	Air bricks
	Cooper's disc
	Doors
	Fires and fireplaces
	Ventilation vents
	Windows

TYPES OF WINDOWS
Attic, bay, bow, casement, dormer, French, louvre, tilted patio windows

EXTRACTOR FANS

UNDERLYING WORKING PRINCIPLE
Blades rotating at high speeds draw stale air from the kitchen using suction. Reverse actions allows some extractor fans to be used to draw in cool air in summer.

CONSTRUCTION
Extractor fans consist of aluminium or plastic boxes covering rotating blades and a powerful electric motor. Fans have a variety of speeds. Fans are operated by a pull cord or switch which opens and closes the shutters.

Position of Extractor Fan

Place the extractor fan away from the main door into the room, and as high on the wall as possible. Rooms without windows must have extractor fans fitted to an external wall or ducted to an external wall.

Care and Cleaning

Disconnect before cleaning. Wash the outside with hot soapy water. Rinse and dry thoroughly.

COOKER HOODS

Construction

Cooker hoods are made from enamelled or stainless steel or copper. A filter removes the grease and cooking smells as air is drawn into the fireproof hood.

Types of Cooker Hoods

Ductless hood: filters remove grease and cooking smells. Air is then recirculated. Generally fitted on internal walls. The metal filters need regular cleaning.

Ducted hood: filters remove stale air. Stale air is conducted along a duct fitted to an external wall. The charcoal or fabric filters need to be replaced at least twice a year.

Air Conditioning

Air conditioning is a combination of heating and ventilation systems driven by a powerful electric fan. Air drawn in is filtered, warmed or cooled and humidified. It is then released into the room or around the house through ducts. These systems require regular servicing.

11

INTERIOR DESIGN AND ROOM PLANNING

ELEMENTS OF DESIGN

The elements of design are:
Colour; Pattern; Texture

COLOUR

Colours can:
- Create a visual unity and visual interest
- Be cool or warm to the eye
- Visually alter the shape/size of a room
- Conceal unattractive features
- Emphasise the best features

Colours terms	Examples
Primary colours	Blue, red, yellow
Secondary colours	Green, orange, purple or violet
Shades	Mixing black with a colour to darken it
Tints	Mixing white with a colour to lighten it
Cool colours	Blue, green
Warm colours	Orange, red, yellow,

COLOUR SCHEMES

Contrasting: colours directly opposite each other
Harmonious: colours next to each other on the colour wheel
Monochromatic: shades or tints of the same colour

PATTERN

Decorative designs that add interest to plain surfaces e.g. carpets, fabrics, objects, are called patterns. Patterns can be created by arranging photographs, objects or furniture. Small patterns suit small rooms, large patterns suit large rooms. Too many patterns create visual clutter.

PATTERNS CAN
- Add interest
- Create atmosphere
- Emphasise a particular feature
- Disguise unattractive features

TYPES OF PATTERNS

Abstract, checks, floral, geometric, motifs, printed textural patterns, self-pattern weaves, stripes, trellis

TEXTURES

Textures can create balance in a room, provide an accent and yet be functional. Textures can be described as:
- Soft or hard
- Smooth or rough
- Matt or shiny
- Absorbing or reflecting light

DESIGN PRINCIPLES

Balance: is the organisation of and relationship between colours, patterns, textures, room lines and shape, proportion and emphasis to produce an attractive setting.

Emphasis: using an object or special area of interest within a room to draw attention to it.

Proportion: is the relationship between the size of the room and all the objects in it.

WALL FINISHES

Bricks or stone, ceramic tiles, cork tiles, paints, mirror tiles, timber panelling or wallpaper.

PAINTS

Composition

Paints consist of:
- Binders to strengthen paint
- Pigments to add colour to paint
- Solvents to help paint spread

Paint types	Composition
Oil-based	Binder, pigment and solvent
Water-based	Plastic binder, powder pigment and water

Characteristics of Paints

Oil-based
- Water resistant
- Hard to use
- Takes long time to dry
- Strong smelling
- Before applying prime surfaces
- Easy to clean surface
- Available in a variety of finishes
- Hard wearing, can be scrubbed
- Clean brushes in spirits

Uses: Bathrooms, kitchens

Water-based
- Easy to use, dries quickly
- Undercoat not always required
- Can be sponged clean, vinyls washable
- Reasonably hardwearing
- Suitable for ceilings, walls
- Special outdoor varieties
- Clean brushes in water

Uses: Ceilings, walls, outdoor varieties

Non-drip Paint
- Can be oil-based or water-based
- Easy to apply
- Covers surfaces quickly
- Colours cannot be mixed

Other paints and products: flame-resistant paint, textured paint, anti-fungal paint, primer, undercoat paint, anti-woodworm treatments

Paint finishes: eggshell, gloss, matt, satin, silk, textured and vinyl emulsion finishes

Creating Pattern and Texture Using Paint

Surface patterns and textures can be created on flat surfaces e.g. walls, floors and furniture using paint finishes such as *stencilling, sponging, ragging* and *stippling*.

Wall coverings	Uses
Paper	
Lining	Uneven walls before painting/papering
Printed	Bedrooms, living rooms, dining rooms
Washable	Family rooms, children's bedrooms
Relief	Self-patterned, use on uneven walls
Woodchip	Use on uneven walls
Vinyl	
Vinyl	Used in all areas
Blown vinyl	Hallways, living rooms
Special effect wallpaper	
Fabric papers	
Flock papers	
Foil paper	

FLOORS AND FLOOR FINISHES

Types of floors	Characteristics and uses
Solid floors	Hard, non-resilient, tiring
	Ground floor in houses
	All floors in apartment blocks
Suspended floors	Resilient, easy underfoot, comfortable
	Ground floors, upper floors

FLOOR FINISHES, PROPERTIES AND USES: TYPES AND PROPERTIES

CORK
- Comfortable and warm
- Quiet underfoot
- Easily marked
- Resilient
- Acid, alkali and water resistant

Uses: sealed for bathrooms, children's rooms and kitchens

TILES
- Clay, ceramic, quarry tiles
- Glazed or unglazed
- Variety in colour and design
- Slippy when wet, dangerous
- Non-slippy variety available
- Hardwearing, easy to clean
- Non-resilient, tiring underfoot, acid, alkali, grease, water resistant

Uses: bathrooms, conservatories, halls, porches, kitchens and utility rooms

VINYL
- Cushioned vinyl and solid vinyl
- Resilient, warm underfoot
- Easy to clean and maintain
- Hardwearing, durable, quiet
- Non-slip when dry, slippy when wet
- Acid, alkali, grease, water resistant

Uses: bathrooms, children's rooms, kitchens, halls and porches

WOODEN
- Resilient, comfortable underfoot
- Durable, hardwearing
- Easy to maintain
- Noisy especially upstairs
- Resistant to acid, alkalis and heat
- Expensive but attractive
- Suitable for asthma sufferers

Uses: bedrooms, children's rooms, dining rooms, halls, living rooms

CARPETS

Classification	Uses
Light domestic	Bedrooms
Medium domestic	Bedrooms, dining rooms
General domestic	Dining rooms, living rooms
Heavy domestic	Halls, landings, stairs, living rooms
Luxury/contract	Hotels, halls, stairs, living rooms

Construction

Bonded: adhesive is used to stick the pile onto backing.

Tufted: pile is stitched into a woven backing, adhesive applied to the backing and a second backing layer holds it in place.

Woven: threads are woven through a jute backing either as separate tufts (Axminster) or as a continuous thread (Wilton).

Fibres Used

Wool, synthetics (acrylic, nylon, polyester, viscose), blends, cotton and silk

Types of pile: cut, looped, sculptured, velvet

Types of underlays: felt, foam, rubber, layered

Advantages of using an Underlay
- Makes carpet last longer, more hardwearing
- Carpet more resilient underfoot
- Provides insulation underfoot
- Reduces noise levels

Factors influencing Choice of Carpets
- Budget available
- Consider cost of carpet, underlay and fitting
- Function of room
- Traffic in room
- Quality of carpet, pile thickness, backing
- Colour, pattern and texture

FURNITURE AND SOFT FURNISHINGS

MATERIALS USED IN FURNITURE
Cane, glass, plastic, metal, textiles and wood

FURNITURE STYLES
- Antique
- Modern
- Traditional

PLASTICS
Composition of Plastics
Consist of air, oil, salt and water

Classification
- Thermoplastic resins

Examples: nylon, PVC
Uses: buckets, vinyl wallpaper, upholstery filling

- Thermosetting resins

Examples: bakelite, melamine, laminated plastics (hard plastics)
Uses: electrical goods, plugs and sockets, fittings (bathroom, kitchen), tableware

Woods
Hardwoods
- Examples: beech, elm, oak, mahogany, teak
- Slow-growing strong trees with fine grains and hard surfaces
- Some hardwoods are expensive e.g. mahogany

Softwoods
- Examples: fir, pine and spruce
- Fast-growing trees with softer, coarser grain
- Cheaper than hardwoods

Man-made Boards
- Chipboard: wood chips glued together
- Hardboard: thin sheets of compressed wood pulp
- Plywood: thin sheets of wood glued together

Wood Finishes
French Polish: solvent, shellac and stain or colour mixed together. Produces a high gloss finish and is damaged easily by alcohol, heat, moisture and perfume.

Wood Stains: oil- or water-based wood colourings that give wood a particular colour e.g. light or dark oak, mahogany, but they do not protect the wood unless added to varnishes.

Wood Varnishes: resins, solvent and a stain mixed together to produce a transparent protective finish.

Wood Finishes:
- Define the colour of the wood, protect the surface, highlight the grain and preserve the wood.

Guidelines for Choosing and Buying Furniture
- Design: attractive, functional, easy to maintain, comfortable
- Construction: well-made joints, smooth finishes
- Budget available (savings/borrowings)
- Cost versus quality
- Materials used: high quality and durable
- Quality symbols and safety symbols
- Guarantees/delivery arrangements
- After sales service

Beds
Types/sizes: single, small double, standard double, queen, king

Mattress and Uses
Foam: cots, bunks, fold-up beds, sofa beds, storage beds
Sprung: divans, single, double and king size, storage beds

Mattress Types
Continuous wire, open springs and pocket springs

Guidelines for Choosing a Bed
- Firm but not too hard, comfortable
- Supports the back
- Longer than the user
- Provides adequate space if shared

Chairs and Tables
Guidelines for Choosing Chairs and Tables

Chairs
- Comfortable, well-designed and constructed
- Supports neck, back and shoulders
- Arms at a comfortable height for users
- Strong legs with grain going downwards

Tables
- Attractive and easy to clean
- Well constructed with secure joints
- Adequately sealed, heat and stain resistant
- A suitable height for the users

Guidelines for Choosing Upholstered Furniture
- Check for symbols of quality, safety, care and maintenance
- Frames should be strong, sturdy and durable
- Foam should be high density to hold its shape
- Upholstered furniture should have closely woven fabric
- Sit on chairs and sofas in the shop before buying
- Check for firmness, support for back, shoulders and neck
- Choose loose covers that can be washed or dry cleaned

SOFT FURNISHINGS

EXAMPLES OF SOFT FURNISHINGS
Bed linen, cushions, curtains, kitchen accessories e.g. tea cosy, oven gloves, loose covers, table linen

FABRICS USED
Natural fibres: cotton, linen, silk, wool
Man-made fibres: acrylics, dralon, polyester

CHARACTERISTICS OF GOOD SOFT FURNISHING FABRICS
- Closely woven and pre-shrunk
- Colour fast, fade resistant
- Drapes well
- Durable and long-lasting
- Easy to care for and maintain
- Flame resistant
- Dirt and stain resistant

ROOM PLANNING
Priorities when Planning a Room
Factors influencing room planning are:
- Cost involved, budget available
- Size and stage of family
- Aspect of room
- Function(s) of room
- Storage requirements
- Existing furniture, new furniture
- Surface finishes
- Services (heating, lighting)
- Traffic flow
- Ease of maintenance
- Safety and hygiene

Planning a Bathroom

Colours: warm colours to counteract clinical bathroom fittings

Floors: comfortable, non-slip, warm underfoot, water resistant e.g. carpets, tiles, vinyl

Furniture: fittings in acrylic or enamelled pressed steel, shower fitment, stool or chair, wall cabinet with lockable door (for medicines)

Walls: tiled half way, tiled shower area, vinyl emulsion paint, vinyl wall covering

Services:
- Heating: radiator/wall-mounted heater specially designed for bathrooms, heated towel rail
- Lighting: central light with switch outside bathroom door, fluorescent light strip near mirror
- Ventilation: extractor fan for bathrooms without a window

Soft furnishings: washable curtains, shower curtains, cotton floor mats

Planning a Bedroom

Colours: warm colours e.g. creams, peach, terracotta, rose

Floors: comfortable, soft and warm underfoot e.g. carpets in warm pale colours

Furniture: comfortable bed, lockers on either side with reading lamps, dressing table with matching mirror and stool, comfortable easy chair or sofa, chest of drawers, built-in wardrobes

Accessories: lamps, cushions, pictures, dried flowers

Walls: emulsion paint in a satin/eggshell finish, wallpaper, spongeable wall covering

Services:
- Heating: radiator(s)
- Lighting: central light, reading or table lamps, light over dressing table
- Ventilation: open the window

Soft furnishings: blinds, lined curtains, matching bedspread and pillowcases, loose cover on chair/sofa/stool, extra cushions on the bed, rug(s)

Planning A Hall, Stairs and Landing

Colours: welcoming colours that suit the aspect of the hall and that link with the rooms leading off the hall and landing.

Floors: comfortable, non-slip, warm underfoot, dirt-resistant, hardwearing, easy to clean e.g. carpets, ceramic or quarry tiles, wooden floors

INTERIOR DESIGN AND ROOM PLANNING

Furniture: hall table, chair(s), central table if space allows, umbrella stand, coat stand

Accessories: pictures, vases of fresh flowers

Walls: vinyl emulsion paint, vinyl wall covering (spongeable)

Services:
- Heating: radiator in hall and on landing
- Lighting: central light in hall, on stairs and on landing, table lamp
- Ventilation: doors and windows

Soft furnishings: blinds and/or curtains, rugs

Planning a Living Room

Colours: warm deep colours that look welcoming at night and during dark winter evenings. Colour co-ordinate fabrics, wall and floor finishes and accessories

Floors: comfortable, warm underfoot, dirt resistant, hardwearing, easy to maintain e.g. carpets or wooden floors

Furniture: best quality sofa, easy chairs, occasional tables, bookcase, display case, storage units, television, stereo

Accessories: pictures, vases of fresh flowers, cushions, photographs

Walls: emulsion paint, spongeable or washable vinyl wallcoverings

Services:
- Heating; radiator(s), open fire (solid fuel or gas)
- Lighting; central light in hall, table lamps, wall lights, display lighting
- Ventilation: doors and windows

Soft furnishings: blinds and/or curtains, cushions, loose covers, rugs

Planning a Dining Room

Colours: warm deep colours on walls, floors and in furniture that allow food to be the focus of the room. Colour co-ordinate fabrics, wall and floor finishes and accessories.

Floors: comfortable, warm underfoot, dirt resistant, easy to clean e.g. carpets or wood

Furniture: best quality comfortable dining room table and chairs, serving table or trolley, display or storage unit

Accessories: pictures, vases of fresh flowers, loose covers on dining chairs

Walls: spongeable emulsion paint, vinyl wall covering

Services:
- Heating: radiator(s), open fire (solid fuel or gas)
- Lighting: central light, table lamps, wall lights
- Ventilation: doors and windows

Soft furnishings: Blinds and/or curtains, loose covers, rug

Planning a Kitchen
Main Priorities to Consider
- Hygiene, safety, services, storage, work triangle, shape of existing room, costs

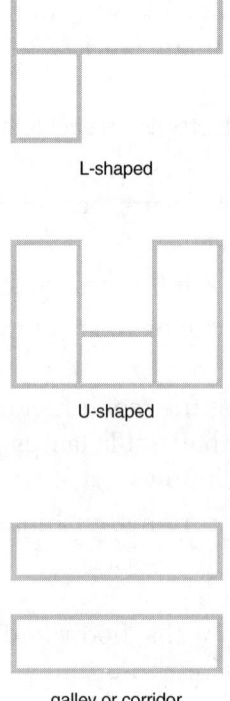

Single-line kitchen: units arranged on one wall only

Galley kitchen: narrow kitchen with units arranged on opposite walls and door/s at the end

L-shaped kitchen: kitchen units arranged on adjacent walls

U-shaped kitchen: kitchen units arranged on three of the four walls

Work Triangle
- Arranged around the fridge, sink and cooker
- Forms the storage, preparation and cooking areas
- An extra large work triangle leads to unnecessary walking
- If too small the work triangle will be cramped

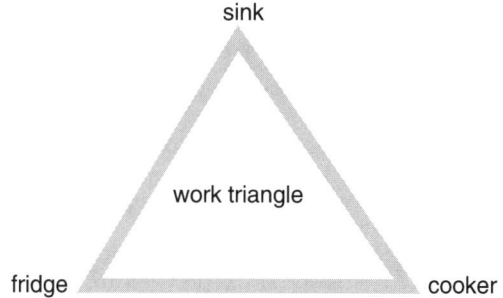

Sequence of Activities in a Kitchen

In the kitchen the work sequence involves:
- Food storage
- Food preparation
- Washing
- Cooking
- Serving

Factors to Consider when Planning a Kitchen
- Budget
- Existing space available
- Layout of new kitchen
- Sink under a window
- Equipment arranged according to area
- Storage requirements for each area
- Position of laundry equipment
- Space for dishwasher, microwave and new pieces of equipment
- Safety, hygiene, electrical, etc.
- Services (heating, lighting and ventilation)
- Extra power points for future requirements
- Kitchen surfaces, easy to clean and maintain, hygienic
- Refuse disposal (bins, waste disposal)

Colours: choose colours that will suit aspect, units, fabrics, wall and floor finishes and accessories, bright, fresh, clear colours

Floors: safe, non-slip when wet, comfortable, warm underfoot, dirt resistant, hardwearing, easy to clean and maintain e.g. vinyl. Quarry tiles are hygienic, but are not resilient and are very tiring underfoot

Kitchen units: choose best quality kitchen units, well designed and easy to clean e.g. floor units, wall units, larder, tall storage cupboard

Other furniture: comfortable, easy to clean kitchen table and chairs

Accessories: clock, photographs/prints, fresh herbs, loose covers on chairs

Walls: spongeable emulsion paint, vinyl wall covering, tiled areas

Services:
- Heating: radiator(s), solid fuel cooker
- Lighting: consider safety at all times central fluorescent light, strip lighting under cupboards
- Ventilation: doors and windows, extractor fan, cooker hood

Soft furnishings: blinds and/or curtains in washable, easy care fabrics

12

HOUSEHOLD APPLIANCES

CLASSIFICATION

- Large appliances
- Small labour-saving appliances
  Appliances using a motor
  Appliances using an element

GUIDELINES FOR CHOOSING APPLIANCES

- Budget available, buy the best you can afford
- Shop around, compare costs, get good value for money
- Buy from a reputable dealer
- Choose a reliable well-known brand name

- Design of appliance, energy-saving features
- Costs involved, purchase, installation and running costs
- Size of household, number of people
- Space available, measure appliance to make sure it fits
- Extra services needed e.g. power points, plumbing, ventilation
- Guarantees and after-sales service

LARGE APPLIANCES

COOKERS

Types of Cookers
- Free-standing cooker
- Built-in split level cooker
- Built-in under worktop cooker
- Solid fuel cooker

Fuels Used
Electricity, gas, oil, solid fuel

Working Principle
Heat for cooking is transferred by conduction, convection and radiation. Temperatures are thermostatically controlled.

Construction of Cookers
The main material used is enamelled steel with fibreglass insulation, consisting of a grill, hob and oven. Cast iron is used in some solid fuel cookers. Hobs usually have four electric radiant rings or electric sealed/solid hotplates. Cookers have one or two ovens with a range of shelving options. Grills are at eye-level or below hob level or built into the main oven.

Some Special Features
Hobs: ceramic hob or halogen ceramic hotplate
Ovens: fan ovens, rotisserie, pyrolytic ovens

Energy Saving features on Cookers
- Dual circuit rings
- Simmerstat rings
- Dual circuit grills
- Stay-clean oven linings
- Auto-timers

Fan Ovens

A fan oven has the element located at the back from where a fan blows the hot air around the oven. There is an even temperature which allows all shelves to be used and results will be the same. Fan ovens are suitable for batch baking. Conventional ovens have uneven temperatures from the top to the bottom shelf.

Use of Cookers
- Follow manufacturer's guidelines
- Never pull or drag pots across ceramic hobs
- Use all cleaners according to the instructions provided
- Use energy-saving features
- Make full use of the oven, cook the entire meal in the oven
- Pre-heat oven before baking
- Time dishes correctly, check a few times
- Make use of residual heat to finish cooking certain dishes
- Avoid opening the oven door during cooking

Care of Cookers
- Turn off main switch before cleaning
- Clean regularly
- Wipe up spills immediately, do not allow to build up
- Avoid marking ceramic hobs, use a special ceramic hob cleaner
- Use oven cleaners according to the manufacturer's instructions

Dishwashers

Capacity
Standard: 12 place settings
Smaller: 6 to 8 place settings

Working Principle
Hot water, forced through rotating spray arms at high pressure, cleans cutlery and dishes. Detergents are used during the cleaning cycle to loosen the food particles. Rinse aid is used to prevent streaking of dishes. Dishes are rinsed using hot water. Residual heat helps to dry the contents of the dishwasher.

Construction of Dishwasher

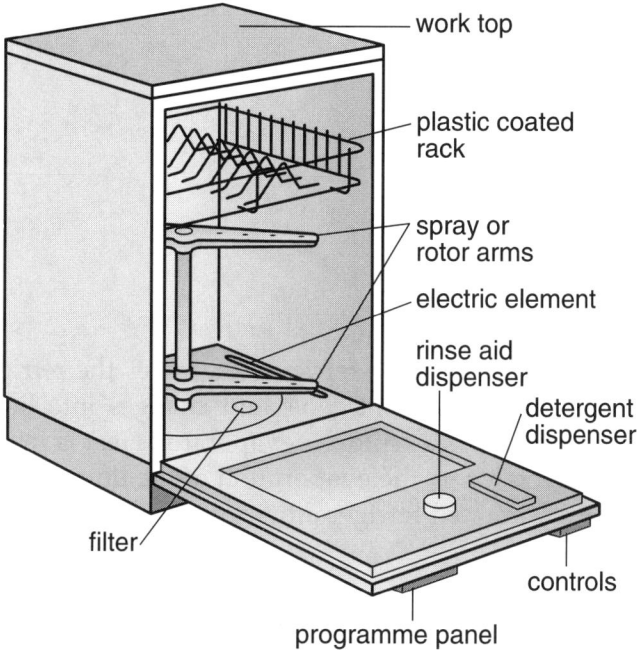

The dishwasher has an outer casing of enamelled steel with an inner casing of stainless steel and a drop down front door opening. Inside there are plastic-coated storage racks, removable cutlery container, a thermostatic water-heating element, motor-driven pump, rotating spray arms and a filter to pick up bits of food. There are dispenser units for salt, detergent and rinse aid.

Use of Dishwasher
- Follow manufacturer's instructions
- Check dishes are dishwasher safe
- Never overload, stack dishes as instructed
- Avoid waste of energy by only using dishwasher when full
- Remove excess food from cutlery, dishes and plates
- Do not use to clean fine crystal, china and silverware
- Use the appropriate programme

Care of Dishwasher
- Use recommended detergent and rinse aids
- Refill rinse aids and water softeners as recommended
- Empty and wash filter regularly
- Wipe outside of dishwasher with warm soapy water

Refrigerators and Freezers

Types of Refrigerator
- Compressor type
- Absorption type

Shapes of Refrigerator
- Standard
- Larder
- Fridge-freezer

Working Principle
The compressor, at the base of the refrigerator, forces the refrigerant into the condenser. The gaseous refrigerant cools and changes into liquid. From the condenser the refrigerant passes into the evaporator. Heat is removed from the food inside the refrigerator by the evaporation of the liquid refrigerant at low temperatures. The evaporated refrigerant returns to the compressor where the cycle begins again.

Construction
Refrigerators consist of an outer layer of insulated enamelled steel with an inner lining of enclosed moulded plastic. Inside are plastic-coated shelving, storage drawers, moulded door storage units and an ice box. An automatic light comes on when the door in opened. Refrigerators also have a thermostat to control temperatures, rubber door seals, a magnetic door catch. The main working parts are the evaporator, condenser, compressor unit and the motor.

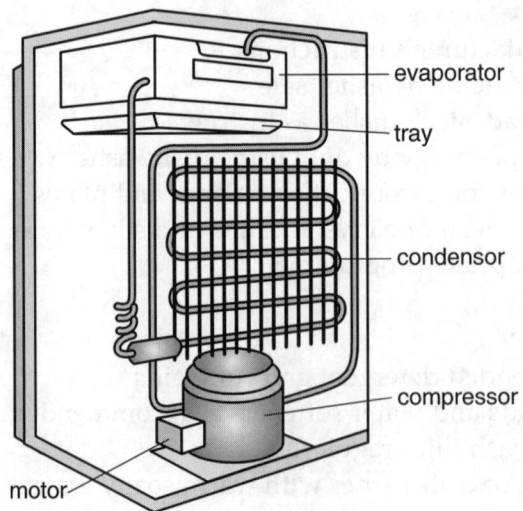

HOUSEHOLD APPLIANCES

Features
- Variety of sizes and shapes
- Adjustable shelving
- Storage drawers
- Door storage for bottles, cartons, etc.
- Ice box or frozen food compartment

Use of Refrigerator
- Follow manufacturer's guidelines
- Open refrigerator only when necessary to avoid energy loss
- Always cool warm/hot food before storing in refrigerator
- Cover foods to avoid flavours being absorbed
- Cover foods to avoid loss of moisture
- Store foods in the recommended area e.g. shelf, storage drawer
- Allow for the circulation of air around food
- Check refrigerator daily to avoid waste

Care of Refrigerator
- Position refrigerator away from any source of heat
- Clean regularly, i.e. weekly
- Wash inside with warm water and breadsoda, never use wash-up liquid or other cleaners
- Wipe the outside of the fridge daily
- Defrost according to the instructions, avoid build up of ice
- Wipe spills immediately, never allow to build up

Methods of Defrosting
- Automatic
- Manual
- Push-button

FREEZERS

Types of Freezers
- Chest freezer
- Upright freezer (tall or under the counter)

Working Principle
Same working principle as for refrigerators. Temperatures are much lower, −18°C. Temperatures within the freezer are lowered to −25,°C when freezing fresh food.

Construction
- Outer casing of enamelled steel with insulated inner lining
- Top or front opening
- Removable plastic-coated shelving or baskets
- Sealed door
- Magnetic door lock
- Thermostat
- Green light (freezer is working normally)
- Orange/red light (freezer temperature is too high)
- Fast freeze switch (lowers temperature for freezing food)

Use of Freezers
- Follow manufacturer's instructions
- Avoid opening the freezer unnecessarily
- Fill to full capacity
- Cool warm or hot foods
- Never freeze more than the recommended capacity
- Turn down temperature well in advance of freezing food
- Label food and use in rotation

Care of Freezers
- Position freezer in a cool place, away from heat
- Defrost as recommended by the manufacturer
- Use the plastic spatula provided to remove excess ice
- Wash with a solution of breadsoda and warm water
- Never open a freezer during a power cut

Star Markings for Refrigerators and Freezers

Diagram	Temperature	Stores
1 Star	−6°C	Frozen food for 1 week
2 Stars	−12°C	Frozen food for 1 month
3 Stars	−18°C	Frozen food for 3 months
4 Stars	−18°C to −25°C	Freeze fresh food and store frozen food for up to 12 months

Washing Machines

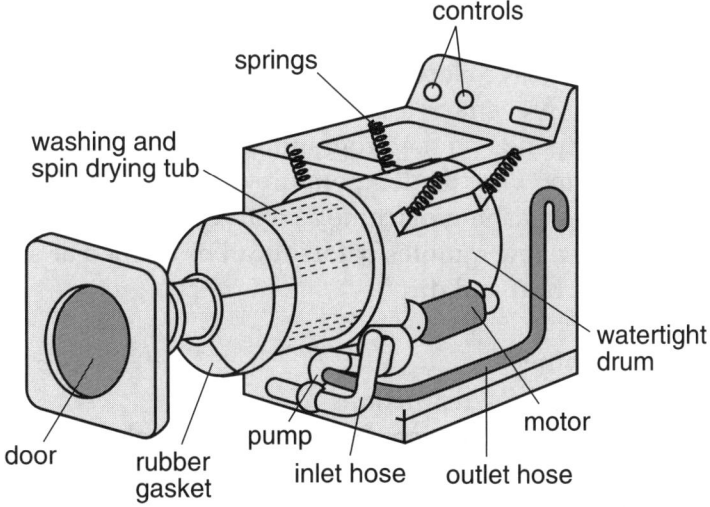

Types
Most homes have an automatic front loader machine. Some homes may have older machines such as single tub or twin tub. A small number of automatic washing machines have an in-built tumble dryer.

Working Principle
Clothes tumble around with detergent and water in a perforated stainless steel drum. The cleaning process loosens and removes the dirt from the clothes. Dirty water is drained away and replaced with clean water a number of times. The final rinsing water is removed from the clothes by the centrifugal high-speed spinning action of the steel drum and pumped from the washing machine. A variety of programmes are available on all machines.

Construction
Washing machines are made of an outer casing of enamelled steel with an inner perforated steel drum enclosed in a water proof drum. Dispensers for detergents and fabric conditioners are located towards the top of the machine. The main working parts are the electric motor, thermostat, water heater, pump and programme selector. A filter removes fluff and loose coins. Inlet and outlet valves control the water. A suspension system holds the drums in place.

Special Features
- *Programme selector*: selection of programmes
- *Easy care wash*: for wools and delicate fabrics
- *Economy button*: to save electricity and water
- *Rinse and hold*: to prevent creasing
- *Spin variation*: depends on the programme selected, can be set manually
- *Temperature selector*: vary the temperature to suit the fabrics
- *In-built dryer*: use washing machine as a dryer
- *Safety lock*: takes a few minutes before it can be opened at end of a wash
- *Filter*: to remove fluff and dirt

Use of Washing Machine
- Follow manufacturer's instructions
- Check the washing instructions on the clothes labels
- Sort according to the labels
- Choose the programme to suit the clothes being washed
- Use the recommended amount of detergent and fabric softener
- Do not mix whites and colours
- Do not overload the machine with too many clothes
- Leave the door ajar after use to dry out the machine and the rubber door seal

Care of Washing Machine
- Remove transit brackets before using machine
- Replace transit brackets before moving machine
- Always check clothes for loose buttons, money, etc.
- Choose the recommended low-foam automatic washing detergent
- Clean filter regularly
- Never force door open or closed, open gently
- Wipe the outside of the machine regularly

DRYERS
Types
- Spin dryer
- Tumbler dryer (condenser dryer, vented dryer)

Working Principles
Spin Dryer
Removes excess water by high-speed rotating centrifugal force. They do not dry clothes.

Tumbler Dryer

A perforated revolving drum through which warm air circulates tumbles and dries the clothes

- In *condenser* dryers, steam from the clothes condenses back into water and is stored in a container, which can be removed when the drying process has been completed.
- In a *vented* dryer the steam is extracted from the rotating drum through a vent linked to an external wall or window.

Construction

Dryers consist of an outer enamelled steel casing with an internal perforated stainless steel drum and a heating element. An external vent removes excess moisture.

Features

- Heat selection button
- Timer
- Reverse action drum
- Capacity 2.5–5 kg.

MICROWAVE OVEN

Working Principle

Electromagnetic waves are directed by a magnetron and rotating blades around the walls of the oven. They penetrate the food to a depth of 2 cm. The water molecules in food vibrate very rapidly creating the heat which cooks or reheats the food. Heat travels to the centre of the food by conduction.

Construction

Microwave ovens consist of an enclosed metal lined steel box, glass door lined with perforated metal mesh, safety lock and seal on door, a magnetron, wave guide or stirrer and a step-up transformer to convert domestic voltage. Some microwave ovens have a turntable.

Use of Microwave Oven

- Read manufacturer's instructions and follow them exactly
- Choose recipes that have been converted for microwave cookery
- Always use suitable containers e.g. glass, special plastics
- Never use metal containers or dishes with metal trims
- Cover food to speed up cooking
- Always allow for the recommended standing time
- Use the recommended heat-resistant cling film

Care of Microwave Oven
- Never turn on oven when empty
- Unplug microwave oven before cleaning
- Wipe around door seal and interior of oven, rinse and dry
- Remove glass turntable, wash in warm soapy water, rinse and dry
- Do not allow spills to build up, wipe up immediately
- Get microwave oven serviced occasionally
- Never use if door is faulty

Advantages
- Economical method of cooking
- Cooks foods quickly, defrosts quickly
- Food retains natural colour, flavour and nutrients
- Saves on washing up, time and energy
- Foods can be served in dishes in which they were cooked
- Ideal for busy families

Disadvantages
- Foods do not brown satisfactorily
- Only suitable for small food items
- Tough cuts of meat cannot be used
- Food poisoning could result if instructions are not followed
- Special dishes must be used
- Dishes need standing time before serving
- Extra time is needed for larger quantities

VACUUM CLEANERS
Types
- Cylinder cleaners
- Upright cleaners
- Combination cleaners and carpet shampooers

Working Principle
A fan driven by an electric motor creates suction, drawing in dirt and dust into a disposable dust bag. Upright vacuum clearers have brushes that beat dirt and dust out of the surface being cleaned. A filtering system reduces the dust particles re-entering the air.

Construction

Vacuum cleaners are made of a metal or plastic outer casing. Usually cylindrical in shape they are mounted on castors. They have a flexible hose with telescopic tubes to which a variety of heads can be attached. The latest designs incorporate sophisticated dust filter systems.

Features
- Variety of heads for different tasks
- Suction control indicator (light, medium and heavy)
- Bag full indicator
- Automatic flex rewind
- Filtering system

Use of Vacuum Cleaners
- Read and follow manufacturer's instructions
- Pick up large items from the floor before vacuuming
- Use the appropriate head for the task
- Remove and replace the dust bag regularly
- Over-filled dust bag reduces efficiency
- Do not pull electric flex when in use

Care of Vacuum Cleaners
- Follow the manufacturer's guidelines
- Replace dust bag and filters as recommended
- Never wash fabric dust bags
- Use disposable bags to line fabric bags, insert as recommended
- Re-wind flex carefully

SMALL LABOUR-SAVING APPLIANCES

ADVANTAGES
- Save time and energy
- Speed up food preparation
- Easily stored
- Not too expensive

SMALL APPLIANCES USING A MOTOR
- Hand-held blender
- Food mixer
- Food processor
- Liquidiser

Small Appliances Using an Element
- Automatic electric kettle (traditional shape and jug kettle)
- Deep fat fryer
- Sandwich toaster
- Slow cooker
- Toaster

General Guidelines for Using Small Appliances
- Follow the manufacturer's instructions exactly
- Never put spoons or fingers near rotating blades, discs
- Slot in the attachments correctly before using
- Slip the blades or disks onto the central spindle
- Use feed tube or fill bowls as recommended
- Fit lids into position
- Use the pulse switch to operate the blades
- Choose the appropriate attachment for the task
- Choose the recommended speed on the appliance
- Use the correct quantities, never overload mixers
- Turn off before removing goblets or bowls

General Guidelines for Care of Small Appliances
- Follow the manufacturer's instructions
- Unplug before cleaning
- Never put parts with motor into water, wipe outside
- Clean blades and discs very carefully
- Dry attachments thoroughly
- Store appliance and attachments in a dry cupboard

Hand-held Blender
Working Principle and Construction
A motor is enclosed in a plastic casing and operated by a pulse button. The pulse button operates the blades which mix the ingredients.
Uses: puréeing baby foods, sauces, soups, fruits, vegetables

Food Mixers
Types
- Standard hand-held mixers
- Larger mixers

Working Principle
A motor drives the rotating beaters or whisks, mixing the ingredients and drawing in air.

Construction
Food mixers consist of an outer casing of metal or plastic with an enclosed electric motor which operates the attachments. Variable speed button controls the beaters or the whisks. Release leavers remove the attachments for cleaning.
Uses: beating, kneading, whisking

FOOD PROCESSORS
Working principle
A motor drives rotating metal/plastic blades and discs. They beat, chop, liquidise, slice and whisk the ingredients in an enclosed metal or plastic container.

Construction
A food processor consists of a motor enclosed in a strong metal or plastic casing and a plastic bowl with a funnelled lid which can be locked in position. It also has a selection of metal and plastic blades, a central spindle to hold blades and discs, and a variable speed button/switch.

LIQUIDISERS
Types
- Stand-alone liquidisers
- Attachments for large food mixers

Working Principle
A motor drives rotating blades at high speed to blend, chop, cut, grind, mix and purée ingredients.

Construction
Rotating metal blades in a glass or plastic goblet are connected to a motor enclosed in a plastic casing. The goblet is removed for washing.

DEEP FAT FRYER
Working Principle
Fat is heated thermostatically by an enclosed element and cooks foods at a variety of settings.

Construction

A heating element, thermostatically controlled, is enclosed between an outer casing of enamelled steel and an inner casing of aluminium. Oil level marks are located on the inside wall of the fryer. A wire basket with a removable handle suspends the food in the oil as it cooks. A pilot light switches off when the oil reaches the correct temperature. Latest designs have special filter systems to prevent frying odours and grease from filling the house.

Guidelines for Use of a Deep Fat Fryer
- Follow manufacturer's instructions exactly
- Pour oil to the recommended level
- Always preheat oil
- Do not put food in until oil is heated
- Lower food gently into the oil
- Never overload the basket

Guidelines for Care of a Deep Fat Fryer
- Read manufacturer's instructions
- Turn off appliance before cleaning
- Strain oil after each cooking session
- Use separate oil for cooking fish, do not mix with other oils
- Always replace oil after using it about eight times
- Strain oil into a container and wipe inside of deep fat fryer
- Clean regularly

ELECTRIC KETTLES

Working Principle
A thermostatically controlled heating element heats water to boiling point and automatically switches itself off.

Construction
A heating element is located at the base of a stainless steel or plastic container. Water level indicators indicate the amount of water in jug kettles. On/off switches control the heating of the water. Cordless kettles are placed on a base. Small amounts of water can be heated in jug and cordless kettles.

Guidelines to Using Electric Kettles
- Follow manufacturer's instructions
- Do not over-fill kettles
- Fill jug kettles by the spout
- Never handle kettle with wet or damp hands

Guidelines for Care of Electric Kettles
- Always unplug before cleaning
- Do not immerse in water
- Wipe the outside of kettle with a damp cloth
- Use a proprietary lime remover if lime builds up

13

CONSUMER EDUCATION

CONSUMER RIGHTS

Consumers have a right to:
- Accurate information
- Quality and choice
- Safe products and services
- Redress (refund, repair, replacement)

CONSUMER RESPONSIBILITIES

Consumers must be:
- Well informed about rights and responsibilities
- Be informed about prices and quality
- Make informed choices
- Examine products and services before purchasing them
- Read labels for information and instructions
- Follow the instructions given on labels
- Use the product for the intended purpose

SOURCES OF CONSUMER INFORMATION

- All forms of Advertising
- Consumer Education e.g. Home Economics
- Information leaflets, brochures
- Labels on product
- Local libraries and resource centres
- Magazines and newspapers
- Shops and showrooms
- Shop assistants and sales staff
- Statutory and voluntary bodies
- The media (television, radio, etc.)
- Word of mouth, family and friends

CONSUMER PROTECTION

Consumers are protected by:
- Legislation and the courts
- Statutory government agencies
- Voluntary agencies

THE CONSUMER INFORMATION ACT 1978

Protects consumers against false information or claims about a price, product or service. It applies to advertisements, shop notices e.g. prices, claims made by sale assistants and information provided on labels.

THE SALE OF GOODS AND SERVICES ACT 1980

A legally binding contract is formed between the buyer and the seller when a product or service is purchased. The Sale of Goods and Services Act 1980 states that the goods or services should be fit for the purpose described, be of merchantable quality, be as described and correspond to any sample on display. This act also applies to guarantees and notices in shops.

UNDER THIS ACT CONSUMERS SHOULD EXPECT
- Service be provided by qualified and skilled people
- Services be provided with due care, diligence and safety
- Sound and merchantable quality materials to be used

Under this act guarantees should

- Be legible and refer to specific goods
- Name the person/company to whom claims can be made
- List the duration of the guarantee from the date of purchase
- Outline the procedure for claiming
- State what the manufacturer will do
- Identify extra charges incurred by the claimant
- Not interfere with the customer's rights

EXAMPLES OF AGENCIES PROVIDING CONSUMER INFORMATION

- European Consumer Information Centre
- Citizens Information Centres
- Consumer Association of Ireland
- Office of the Director of Consumer Affairs
- Government Departments
- The Ombudsman
- Food Safety Authority of Ireland

The Office of the Director of Consumer Affairs

The Director of Consumer Affairs:

- Informs consumers about their rights and responsibilities
- Enforces consumer laws, initiates legal proceedings against offenders
- Enforces advertising standards, product labelling
- Oversees safety and price displays
- Aims to raise all standards relating to goods and services

The Ombudsman

Deals with unresolved complaints against government departments and offices e.g. Health Boards, Local Authorities, An Post and Telecom Éireann.

National Social Services Board

The NSSB provides consumer information about services available and supports the Citizens' Information Centres. It also advises the Minister for Health on the development of the social services.

Small Claims Courts

Complaints dealing with small claims can be dealt with by the local District Court. The claim must not exceed £600. Complaints are dealt with quickly, informally, without a solicitor, by the Registrar who tries to settle the dispute before referring the matter to the court.

Voluntary Non-statutory Agencies

Consumer Association of Ireland Ltd.

This is a non-profit, independent organisation representing Irish consumers. It provides consumer information and works towards improving consumer legislation. A monthly magazine, *Consumer Choice*, provides information on a variety of products and services available in Ireland.

Trade and Professional Organisations/Associations

Higher standards are encouraged among members of such associations.

SHOPPING

Points to Consider when Buying Products and Services
- Make a shopping list and stick to it
- Never shop for food when hungry
- Avoid impulse buying
- Buy from a reliable source
- Shop locally if possible to save travel costs
- Examine the design, labels, 'sell-by' dates
- Guarantees and after sales service
- Suitability for purpose
- Buy the best quality you can afford
- Value for money, compare prices
- Check receipts before leaving the shop
- Store receipts, guarantees and instruction

Types of shops	Examples
Chain stores	Dunnes Stores, Penneys
Discount shops	£1 shops
Department stores	Arnotts, Clerys, Shaws
Independent local shops	The local shop
Large Shopping Centres	Tallaght, Blanchardstown
Multiple chain stores	Dunnes Stores, Marks and Spencers
Supermarkets	Dunnes Stores, Superquinn
Voluntary chain stores	Centra, Spar
One-Stop-Shops	Petrol stations/shops
Hyper Markets	Very large shopping centres or areas

SHOPPING TERMINOLOGY

Bulk buying: buying large amounts of an item so that it works out cheaper. It is only good value when it is an item that will be used

Loss leaders: selling a small number of items at cost price to encourage consumers to buy in that particular shop

Own brands: items packaged simply and inexpensively, marked with the company logo and sold cheaper than other leading brands

Special offers: small number of items sold as special offers each week to attract customers

Receipts: records of items bought and money paid. Keep receipt as proof of purchase

Store Club Cards: customers use swipe cards to check in when paying bills. Credits or points are given which when added up can provide the consumer with money vouchers or other items

Unit pricing: cost per unit e.g. per kilogram

LABELLING

TYPES OF LABELLING
- Care labels
- Date stamping
- Food labelling
- Company Logos and symbols
- Manufacture's information
- Manufacturer's instructions
- Safety Labels

FOOD LABELLING

A number of EU regulations and the Consumer Information Act 1978 outline the information that must be provided on food labels. Information provided on pre-packed food includes:
- Country of origin
- Name and address of manufacturer
- Name of product
- Weight of product
- Expiry date or best before date
- Ingredients in descending order
- Preparation and cooking instructions

- Storage instructions
- Nutritional information
- Irradiation must be indicated

Non-prepacked food information on notices should include origin, class and variety (fruits and vegetables) and cost per kilogram.

TEXTILE CARE LABELS INFORMATION

Drying instructions: dry flat; drip dry; do not tumble dry; line dry; tumble dry

Ironing instructions: do not iron; cool iron; warm iron; hot iron

Dry-cleaning: do not dry-clean; dry-cleaning processes (symbols A, P, F)

QUALITY MARKS

Symbols and marks indicate the quality and safety of products and services. These include:
Approved Quality System, Communauté Europeanne, Caighdeán Éireannach, The Kitemark, British Standards Institute, Flame Resistant and Doubly Insulated mark

WARNINGS SYMBOLS

Symbols to indicate:
- corrosive, flammable, harmful and irritant or toxic substances

14

MONEY MANAGEMENT

TERMINOLOGY

Gross income: the amount of money we earn before deductions (tax, etc.).

Net income: the amount of money left, following compulsory and voluntary deductions.

PAYE: pay as you earn tax deduction system, employers deduct the tax from the employees' salary or wages and return the tax to the Revenue Commissioners.

PRSI: pay-related social insurance, payable by employed persons 16–66 years. It enables employees to claim social welfare benefits under certain criteria.

Family income: salaries, wages, family allowance, interest on savings and investments and pensions.

Family Income Support Supplement: 'FIS' supplement is a tax-free payment to help a family if the family income falls below a certain limit.

Child Benefit Payment: a monthly payment by the Department of Social Welfare in respect of each child up to 16 years and up to 18 years if in full-time education.

Supplementary Welfare Allowance: this is a weekly allowance, provided for eligible people who have little or no income.

All wages and salaries are taxed according to criteria set out by the Revenue Commissioners. Allowances are given and deductions then made accordingly. Tax Rates, Bands and Tables outline the tax arrangements made in the budget each year. They are subject to change, so check them out in the year in which you sit the Leaving Certificate Examination.

MAIN TAX ALLOWANCES

- Single, married, widowed person, dependant relative, incapacitated persons (employing a carer)
- PAYE allowance
- VHI (allowance on premiums paid in previous year)
- Work expenses
- One-parent family (single person, widowed person)
- Age allowance (single, married)
- Covenants
- Dependents (dependent relative, incapacitated child)
- PRSI

EXAMPLES OF TAX ALLOWANCES, RELIEFS AND INCOME

- Special tax allowance for long-term unemployed taking up a job
- Widowed parent allowance (Bereavement Allowance)
- Mortgage interest
- Fees paid to Approved Colleges
- Relief for fees paid for training courses
- Non-PAYE income and benefits-in-kind

LEVIES

- Health
- Employment

EXAMPLES OF DEDUCTIONS FROM SALARY/WAGES

- Income tax
- Government levies
- Superannuation
- PRSI
- Health Insurance
- Savings e.g. Credit Union, National Instalments Savings
- Union subscription

EXAMPLES OF SOCIAL WELFARE PAYMENTS AND ALLOWANCES

Payments	Examples of Benefits
PRSI contributions	Unemployment benefit
	Contributory old-age pension
	Maternity benefit
Assistance payments	One-parent family payment
	Non-contributory pension
Universal benefits	Child benefit
	Pensioners' free travel

BUDGETING: A PLAN FOR MANAGING MONEY

REASONS FOR BUDGETING

- Develops good money management habits
- Reduces financial worry and stress
- Balances expenditure and income
- Controls expenditure
- Plans for irregular and regular bills
- Reduces unnecessary spending e.g. impulse spending

- Includes short- and long-term saving goals
- Leads to security and independence

PLANNING A BUDGET: GENERAL GUIDELINES

Item	Suggested	Examples
Shelter	25–30%	Rent/mortgage, insurance, repairs
Food	25%	A healthy balanced diet
Household	20%	Heating, cooking, lighting, telephone
Health	5%	Medical insurance, dentist, doctor
Transport	5–7%	Depends where you live, work, type of transport
Savings	5%	Long-term, short-term, insurance, emergencies
Clothing	5%	Clothes, dry cleaning, shoes
Personal/ entertainment/ leisure	5%	Nights out, sports, holidays, gifts

BUDGETS NEED TO BE

- Re-organised as family needs/priorities change
- Examined as income changes e.g. employment/unemployment
- Checked annually

SAVING SCHEMES

When considering saving schemes check out:
- Ease of withdrawal
- Rate of interest
- Security arrangements
- Tax payable
- Other benefits

SUMMARY OF SAVING OPTIONS/SCHEMES

Institution	Examples
Bank	Deposit account
	Investment bonds and funds
	Term account
Building Society	Bonus account
	Building Society Bonds
	Deposit/Share account
	Special Savings Account
Credit Union	Savings/Share account
An Post	Children's savings account
	Deposit account
	National Instalments Savings
	Saving Certificates
	Saving Bonds

USING CREDIT 'BUYING NOW, PAYING LATER'

Credit is the provision of money to allow consumers to buy goods or services and to repay the money along with interest and other charges.

LEGISLATION

The Consumer Credit Act 1995 regulates consumer credit arrangements. A consumer is defined as 'a person acting outside his trade, business or profession'. The Consumer Credit Act, 1995 requires that the Annual Percentage Rate (APR) of charge be shown in advertisements and agreements.

ADVANTAGES OR BENEFITS TO THE CONSUMER

- Use of goods while paying for them
- Can buy large expensive items e.g. home, car
- Can buy luxury items e.g. holiday
- Do not need to save, low initial cost
- Little need to carry large sums of cash
- Credit-free period on budget accounts and credit cards

DISADVANTAGES

- Goods can be repossessed if repayments are not made
- Goods not owned by consumer until final instalment is paid
- Expensive as interest rates are high
- Easy to overspend when buying on credit
- May lead to financial problems if not managed

CREDIT AGREEMENTS

When entering into credit agreements ensure that agreements are in writing, provide names and addresses of all the parties, and be signed by all the parties to the agreement. They should include details of cost penalties which apply if the consumer does not comply with the terms of the agreement.

A copy of the agreement must be given to the consumer on completion or within 10 days of that date. Consumers may withdraw from the agreement within 10 days of receiving a copy of it by providing written notice to the creditor. This is called the cooling-off period.

HIRE PURCHASE AGREEMENTS

Hire purchase agreements must identify the agreement as 'hire purchase', provide names and address of the parties, description of goods, details of hire purchase price, instalments arrangements, cash price of goods, information on termination of agreement, recovery of goods by owner, details of penalty clause and cooling off period.

EXAMPLES OF CREDIT BUYING

- Bank overdraft and loans
- Budget accounts in large stores
- Charge cards
- Credit card
- Hire purchase

INSURANCE

Types	Examples
Assurance	Endowment assurance
	Life assurance
	Term assurance
	Whole life assurance
Insurance	Car insurance
	Health insurance (VHI, BUPA, group schemes)
	Household contents
	Personal valuables e.g. jewellery, video camera
	House insurance (building)

BENEFITS TO CONSUMER
- Tax relief may be possible
- Savings may be built in as part of some schemes
- Caters for difficult times e.g. illness, death, inability to work, robbery
- Provides a sense of financial security

MAIN DISADVANTAGE
- Some types may be expensive

METHODS OF PAYING FOR GOODS AND SERVICES

- Cash
- Cheque with matching bankers' card
- Credit card e.g. Access, Visa, Mastercard
- Laser card
- Store Budget Cards
- e-commerce on Internet

PART II B
SOCIOLOGY

15

FAMILY, RELATIONSHIPS AND MARRIAGE

THE FAMILY

TERMINOLOGY

FAMILY
A small group of people related by blood, marriage or adoption who generally share the same home

FAMILY OF ORIGIN
The family in which we grow up

FAMILY OF PROCREATION
The families which we form as adults in order to have our own children

TYPES OR FAMILY STRUCTURES

EXTENDED FAMILY:
A large number of relations, many generations, living together in the same neighbourhood

NUCLEAR FAMILY:
Parents and their children with no relations living close by.

SOME CHARACTERISTICS OF THE EXTENDED FAMILY

The extended family is:
- Located in areas where social change is slow
- Based on the traditional family structure
- Large in size, many relatives, many generations
- Located in one area, one house or houses close together
- A large family (provides an economic advantage)
- Long-lasting and reliable in a crisis
- Based on clearly defined roles for all members
- Divided into clearly defined social divisions
- Authoritarian in control and patriarchal

SOME CHARACTERISTICS OF THE NUCLEAR FAMILY

The nuclear family is:
- Located in areas of rapid social change
- Accepting of change more easily than the extended family
- Based on a modern family structure
- Small in size (parent(s) and children only)
- Mobile, moves for a variety of reasons e.g. careers
- Economically dependent on a small number of people
- Subject to change in family structure
- Based on flexible roles for all family members
- Independent, democratic and egalitarian
- Less reliable in a crisis, more isolated from extended family
- Short lived, children move away from home

THE FUNCTIONS OF FAMILY

NURTURING FUNCTION
The family cares for the emotional and psychological development of the child, providing reassurance, encouragement, love and security.

EDUCATIONAL FUNCTION
The family is the first location for early learning. It later supports the state education of children by supervising homework, praising and encouraging the child to work to the best of her/his ability.

Cultural or Socialisation Function
The family is the primary centre of socialisation. It introduces the child to the beliefs, culture, language(s), norms, traditions and values of the society in which they live.

Protective Function
Families protect and care for the young, elderly and individuals with special needs.

Reproductive Function
By having children families ensure the survival of the human race. The family structure also regulates sexual activity within society.

Economic Function
Individuals within the family work to earn money to provide for the members of the family.

SOME CHANGES AFFECTING THE FAMILY

Family is influenced by:
- Trends in marriage e.g. marriage breakdown
- New legislation relating to marriage
- Size of families
- Educational developments/opportunities
- Families moving residence more frequently
- Family functions shared with the state
- Improvement in living conditions and nutrition
- Changes in the roles and expectations
- People living longer
- Employment and unemployment
- Leisure as part of lifestyle
- Influence of the media, advertising
- Travel, experiencing other cultures
- Technological developments, Internet

MARRIAGE: CHANGES IN IRELAND

There is a reduction in the number of people getting married. People are completing their education, organising a career and are older getting married. Some couples are not getting married but choose to live together. There is an increase in marriage breakdowns, one-parent families and second families. A decrease has occurred in family size. The media has influenced marriage and family life.

LEGISLATION: NEW LAWS

In Ireland new laws relating to marriage, to the protection of children, The Family Law (Divorce) Act 1996 and other legislation, are bringing about changes in family life.

FAMILY SIZE AND THE MODERN FAMILY

The reduction in the size of the Irish family has been influenced by:
- Economic factors, large mortgages
- Birth control
- The changing role of women in the world
- Women remaining in, or returning, to the workplace

EDUCATION

Because of compulsory education, young people are remaining in the system longer and, as a result, they are staying at home with their families until they are older. There are opportunities for adults to return to full-time education. Retraining is also available for individuals who want to return to the workforce. Lifelong learning is becoming part of everyone's life.

WOMEN AND FAMILY

Some women work full-time in the home, while others combine working in the home with full-time employment outside the home. Women are less dependent than in the past and their roles are changing. Their salaries supplement the family income or provide the only income. Partners may be unemployed or they may be raising children on their own. Many women want to continue working outside the home. They want to develop careers alongside raising children.

DIFFICULTIES FACING DUAL-CAREER WOMEN

- Organising suitable safe child care
- Cost of child care
- Finding flexible jobs that can fit in with the demands of family
- Feelings of guilt, becoming stressed and unable to cope
- Managing two jobs (home and outside work)
- Balancing career opportunities with demands of family life
- Development of tension between partners, marriage problems
- Little help at home from partner

FULL-TIME HOMEMAKERS

Women and men are sharing the work of the home more than in the past. Roles are less defined. Today a number of men are working full-time in the home and their partners work outside the home. Full-time Homemaker refers to both men and women who are in the home on a full-time basis.

DIFFICULTIES FACED BY FULL-TIME HOMEMAKERS
- Homemaking is considered low-status work
- No previous training for the task
- Financially dependent on their partner
- Loneliness and isolation
- Repetitive tasks, no challenges

THE DUAL-CAREER FAMILY

Because of the changes taking place in society, both parents frequently work outside the home. The dual-career family depends on good communication between partners, flexibility, adaptability and a shared approach to homemaking and care of children.

ADVANTAGES OF DUAL-CAREER FAMILY
Financial Benefits
- Improves the standard of living, increases family income
- Provides financial security for those with large mortgages
- Extra money pays for luxuries e.g. holidays

Social Benefits
- Partners can enjoy the status conferred by outside employment
- Opportunities for training and development
- Adult company and social life outside the family
- Provides financial security for the future

DISADVANTAGES OF DUAL-CAREER FAMILY

Problems faced by the dual-career family include organising child-care, costs of child-care, feelings of guilt, the demands of home and work, stress and exhaustion. Families have to get up extra early to travel to carer. Tension between parents sometimes results. There is very little time available for good communication and decision making.

LONE PARENT FAMILY

Individuals may be raising children on their own because of death, desertion, divorce, parent in prison, separation or unplanned pregnancy.

DIFFICULTIES FACED BY LONE PARENT FAMILY
- Finding suitable and affordable housing
- Lack of child-care facilities, cost involved
- Managing home and employment
- Financial problems
- Isolation and loneliness
- Stigma associated with partner in prison
- Social isolation

ROLES AND RELATIONSHIPS

THE HUSBAND–WIFE RELATIONSHIP
- Is an equal partnership
- Is an exclusive intimate relationship that excludes others
- Emphasises friendship and open communication
- Demands fidelity, honesty, maturity and responsibility
- Requires active listening
- Is based on sharing of the traditional roles and new roles
- Requires the ability to love, to receive love, to share and to forgive

CHILD–PARENTS RELATIONSHIP
- Is the most important first relationship
- Depends on parents' ability to care for and love children
- Emphasises honesty, justice, loyalty and maturity
- Develops warm relationships and a sense of responsibility
- Provides praise, security, approval and acceptance
- Develops self-esteem and confidence in the child

SIBLING (BROTHERS, SISTERS) RELATIONSHIPS
- Can be close relationships
- Can create difficulties when siblings compete
- Allows older children to be role models
- Prepares them for life outside the family
- Develops listening, communication and co-operation skills

GRANDCHILDREN–GRANDPARENTS RELATIONSHIPS

- Very special relationships, generally good
- Can last a short or long time
- Grandparents have more time than parents
- Less rules and regulations in place, more informal
- Grandchildren learn respect for older people
- Grandchildren learn to communicate and negotiate
- Problems may arise between parents and grandparents in relation to the rearing of children

SOME RIGHTS AND RESPONSIBILITIES WITHIN THE FAMILY

- Parents must provide for all the needs of their children: education, love, understanding, a warm and caring environment, security, protection from all forms of abuse and discrimination, provide appropriate specialised care for children with special needs
- Partners must fulfil rights and responsibilities to each other
- Children have a responsibility to care and respect each other
- Children have a responsibility to care and respect their parents

MARRIAGE

TERMINOLOGY

SOCIAL INSTITUTIONS
Social order is based on social institutions. Social institutions have established acceptable patterns of behaviour. Marriage is one of the social institutions.

MARRIAGE
Marriage is a legal and social union between men and women that regulates sexual and child-rearing functions within a framework of companionship and economic co-operation. The institution of marriage is governed within each cultural group by specific regulations in regard to the number of partners, excluded/restricted relationships, residence, property and inheritance, rights, responsibilities and legislation.

NUMBER OF PARTNERS IN A MARRIAGE
Monogamy: only one partner for each spouse
Polygamy: a spouse may have more than one partner
Polyandry: permits one woman to have more than one husband
Polygyny: allows one man to have more than one wife
Cohabitation: two unmarried people, living together and sharing a home

Restricted Relationships
Relationships excluded under marriage include:
- Affinity or related by marriage e.g. woman may not marry her stepfather, etc.
- Consanguinity or blood relationships e.g. woman may not marry her father, etc.

Location of Residence
Couples may choose to live on their own or with parents
Matrilocal: living with the parents of the female
Neolocal: couple setting up home on their own
Patrilocal: living with the parents of the male

Rights and Obligations of Partners within Marriage
- Legally, partners must live together
- Each partner has the right to the company of the other
- Partners are entitled to fidelity and loyalty
- Marriages must be consummated
- Partners have joint guardianship of children
- Partners are legally obliged to provide for their children

PREPARING FOR MARRIAGE
Attitudes to marriage are moulded by experiences in our homes and the communities where we live.

Education in the Home and Community
The home is the first experience of marriage, whether the home life is happy or unhappy, for individuals. This experience influences attitudes to marriage and approaches to relationships. Experience of marriage is gained also within community, from friends and images of families in the media.

Pre-marriage Courses
Pre-marriage courses are run by the Catholic Marriage Advisory Council and the Marriage Counselling Service (non-denominational) for couples planning to get married. Topics ranging from communication, expectations of marriage, finance, home management, relationships, sex, family planning and parenthood are covered by a team of experts.

Advantages of Marriage Preparation Courses
Such courses:
- Provide information about legal requirements
- Allow individuals to discuss their expectations of marriage
- Raise and explore problems that face married couples
- Provide a forum for couples to discuss differences

Education in School
Individual subject areas e.g. Religious Studies, Home Economics, Lifeskills, provide opportunities for discussions on relationships, marriage and family life.

CHURCH MARRIAGES IN IRELAND

Church marriages take place with the clergyman performing the roles of priest and of clerk of the registry office. After the ceremony the couple sign the register, witnessed by two people (one witness satisfies state legal requirements) and by the priest. The signing now generally takes place in front of all the wedding guests.

THE MARRIAGE CONTRACT IN IRELAND (LEGAL CONDITIONS)

- Marriage must be voluntary
- Partners must be of the opposite sex
- Partners must not be closely related
- Only one partner is allowed, monogamy
- Marriage age is restricted to over 18 years
- Marriages between individuals under 18 must obtain permission from the Circuit Court
- Three months advance notice must be given to the relevant District Registrar
- Ceremonies must be held in a registered place in the presence of a recognised person
- Couples must sign the legal register witnessed by one other person
- Following a church ceremony the presence of two witnesses is to satisfy a church ruling

Registered places: church, registry office or synagogue
Recognised persons: priest, minister or an appointed person

SUMMARY OF CIVIL MARRIAGES IN IRELAND

- The couple must apply for a district registrar's licence or certificate
- Couples living in different districts must notify the registrar of each district
- The ceremony takes place in a registry office
- The ceremony is performed by an appointed person
- Civil marriages satisfy the legal state requirements

LEGISLATION RELATING TO MARRIAGE AND FAMILY

Laws relating to marriage in Ireland include:
- The Family Law (Miscellaneous Provision) Act 1997
- Children's Act 1997
- The Family Law (Divorce) Act 1996
- Domestic Violence Act 1996
- Family Law Act 1995
- Judicial Separation Act 1989 (considerably amended by Family Law Act 1995)
- Family Home protection Act 1976
- Family Law (Maintenance of Spouses and Child) Act 1976

LIFE CYCLE OF A MARRIAGE

Marriages go through a series of stages or cycles. These include the early years or honeymoon stage, child-rearing stage, leaving home stage (further education or work), pre-retirement stage, planning for retirement and retirement.

MARRIAGE STABILITY

Factors influencing marriage stability include:
- Maturity and responsibility, honesty
- Common background, education and areas of interest
- High self-esteem and confidence
- Ability and willingness to share
- Good communication and negotiation skills
- Shared responsibility for children
- Respect for the freedom and rights of others
- Accepting differences in others, accommodating their needs
- Knows oneself, accepts and controls emotions

MARRIAGE INSTABILITY

Factors causing instability in marriage might include:
- Pregnancy before marriage
- New baby very early into the marriage, couple unprepared
- Inadequate preparation for the marriage
- Conflict because of cultural, racial, religious and role differences
- Emotional immaturity, incompatibility
- Violence within the home against spouse and/or children
- Problems associated with alcohol, drug abuse, gambling
- Career pressures, spouse spends more time at work
- Career expectations and changing role of women
- Unemployment, short-term and long-term
- Financial e.g. large mortgage or other loans

EFFECTS OF MARITAL BREAKDOWN

ON PARTNERS/SPOUSES
- Inability to cope with the changes
- Unable to deal with tasks done by other partner e.g. banking
- Emotional problems e.g. feeling of guilt, hostility
- Loneliness and insecurity, new single status
- Loss of family and friends (taking of sides)
- Financial insecurity and stress
- Sorting out the legal issues e.g. custody of children
- Selling of home, changing community and location
- Alcohol or drug dependence

ON CHILDREN
- Difficulty in adjusting to new situation
- Loss of one parent from the home
- Behavioural difficulties resulting from the emotional turmoil and losses
- Caught emotionally between two parents, divided loyalty
- Feelings of insecurity and even loss of friends
- Moving house, location, even school
- May experience loss of family, grandparents, cousins
- Change in image of family life, may be distorted

ON GRANDPARENTS
- May be unwelcome in the new home
- Could loose contact with grandchildren
- Might be unhappy about second relationships

On Community/Society
- Increase in one parent families
- New second families
- Increased demands on welfare services and housing
- Changes in the social order of communities and society
- Behavioural problems among young people
- Problems at work e.g. illness, absenteeism

THE END OF A MARRIAGE

Marriages can end through the death of a spouse, annulment, separation or divorce.

NULLITY

A decree of nullity declares that a valid marriage never existed because of a particular defect in one or both individuals. Some of the defects that are recognised as invalidating a marriage include: individual was drunk or on drugs at the time of the marriage, homosexuality, non-consummation of marriage and an inability on the part of a partner or the partners to develop normal marital relationships.

DIVORCE

Marriages can be legally ended in Ireland through divorce. The right to remarry has been provided for partners. Provision is made for the support of the spouse and children and the custody of children.

MARRIAGE COUNSELLING SERVICES

Marriage counselling services aim to help couples stay together, work through their problems, find solutions and prevent a breakdown of the marriage.
Examples: Marriage Counselling Service and the Catholic Marriage Advisory Council

FAMILY MEDIATION SERVICE

This is a free State service. It aims to help couples organise their separation in terms of custody of children, access to children for non-custodial parent, maintenance for spouse and children, division of property.

16

PROBLEMS IN FAMILIES, COMMUNITIES AND SOCIETY

BEREAVEMENT/DEATH

Coping with a death in a nuclear family without the support and care of an extended family can be a difficult and a very lonely experience.

EFFECTS OF DEATH ON SPOUSE, FAMILY AND SOCIETY

ON THE SPOUSE OR PARTNER
- Loneliness, intense sense of loss
- Economic problems due to inadequate financial provision
- Death of breadwinner, only wage earner
- Tackling unfamiliar jobs e.g. paying bills, banking, shopping
- Dependency on sedatives or alcohol
- Need for bereavement counselling

ON THE FAMILY/CHILDREN
- Unable to come to terms with the loss
- Loneliness, emotional problems
- Worry about money, the future
- Worry about the other parent
- Personality development may be damaged
- Need for bereavement counselling

ON COMMUNITY/SOCIETY
- Establishment of Bereavement Counselling Service
- Need to care for neighbours, family and friends

SUPPORT SERVICES/GROUPS

Bereavement Counselling Services, Bereaved Parents Association, Bethany Support Group, National Association of Widows in Ireland

CHILD ABUSE

Child abuse ranges from emotional, physical or sexual abuse of children by parents, siblings or others outside the immediate family.

EFFECTS OF ABUSE ON CHILD, FAMILY AND SOCIETY

ON THE CHILD
- Emotional, intellectual and physical development delayed/impaired
- Poor self-esteem, little confidence
- Feelings of shame leading to depression
- Fear, stress, insecurity
- May accept abuse as normal behaviour
- Could become abusers in the future

ON THE FAMILY
- Cycle of violence established as a norm within the family
- Unhappy family atmosphere, family breakup
- Anger and bitterness

ON COMMUNITY/SOCIETY
- More neglectful and violent society
- Lowering of respect for others
- Instability in relationships
- Higher rates of family breakup
- Increased demands on welfare services

SUPPORT SERVICES/GROUPS

Parents under Stress, Childline, Irish Society for the Prevention of Cruelty to Children, Health Boards. Legislation, Child Care Act 1991, makes provision for Health Boards to take action when children are not receiving appropriate care and protection.

CRIME AND JUVENILE DELINQUENCY

Breaking the law of the state is a crime. Deviants are individuals who break the laws of the state. Provisions in the form of special schools and rehabilitation institutes are in place for dealing with children and young people who break the law.

FACTORS CONTRIBUTING TO CRIME

- Substance abuse e.g. drugs
- Family background, lack of control in the home
- Lack of accountability to parents
- Long-term unemployment
- Poor self-image, self-esteem, little confidence
- Low educational achievements, doing badly at school
- Homelessness or poor housing conditions
- Excitement, peer pressure

TYPES OF CRIMES

INDICTABLE OFFENCES
The most serious offences, individuals are brought to court and if convicted are fined or imprisoned

NON-INDICTABLE OFFENCES
The less serious offences

EFFECTS OF CRIME ON INDIVIDUALS, FAMILY AND SOCIETY

ON INDIVIDUALS
- Imprisonment, loss of freedom
- Stigma, rejection by society
- Criminal record, unemployment because of record
- Emotional, personal problems, low self-esteem

ON THE FAMILY
- Rejection by community, social stigma
- Poor role models within family
- Rejection of the criminal by family
- Spilt loyalties within the family
- Forced to move house, fear

ON COMMUNITY/SOCIETY
- Increased criminal activity
- Anxiety and fear on the part of citizens
- De-stabilises communities
- Anger when sentences are lenient or criminals are not charged
- Increase in cost of security systems on homes and businesses

- Increased costs to the tax payer
- Victim support is needed

SUPPORT SERVICES/GROUPS

Counselling, Prison system, Juvenile Liaison Scheme, Probation and Welfare Service of the Department of Justice, Rehabilitation Schools, National Office of Victim Support, Victim/Witness Programme.

MARITAL VIOLENCE

Emotional, physical and sexual violence are crimes. Victims of these crimes need protection from the perpetrators.

FACTORS CONTRIBUTING TO MARITAL VIOLENCE

- Emotional immaturity, lack of emotional control
- Need to control and dominate others
- Alcohol abuse
- Poverty, economic difficulties
- Unemployment
- Abusers were themselves abused as children

EFFECTS OF MARITAL VIOLENCE ON SPOUSE, FAMILY AND SOCIETY

ON THE SPOUSE
- Depression, low self-esteem
- Feelings of guilt
- Physical pain, fear for ones life
- Intense emotional distress and damage
- Fear for the safety and welfare of children

ON THE FAMILY/CHILDREN
- Emotional disturbance and distress
- Constant fear and anxiety
- Family breakup
- Acceptance by children of violent behaviour as the norm
- Children might become abusers in the future
- Insecurity and unhappiness

PROBLEMS IN FAMILIES, COMMUNITIES AND SOCIETY

On Community/Society
- Increase in dysfunctional families
- More adults and children dependent on welfare services
- Undermining of society

SUPPORT SERVICES/GROUPS
Domestic Violence and Sexual Assault Unit of an Garda Siochána, Women's Aid, Family Aid, National Office of Victim Support.

GAMBLING

Gambling is an addiction or compulsive behaviour that provides excitement for the gambler even though they may loose large amounts of money.
Examples: card games, dog racing, horse racing, lottery tickets and slot machines

EFFECTS OF GAMBLING ON INDIVIDUALS, FAMILY AND SOCIETY

On individuals
- Economic problems, borrowing from others
- Loss of home and other assets
- Breakdown of relationships, family breakdown
- Resorting to criminal activities e.g. stealing from employer
- Absenteeism from work and family
- Emotional problems, depression, guilt

On the Family/Children
- Financial difficulties, unable to pay bills
- Loss of family home
- Breakdown in relationships, breakup of family
- Instability, violence in the home, fear
- Emotional anxiety for family members

On Community/Society
- Increases demands on welfare services
- Increase in criminal activities, fraud, stealing
- Social welfare payments used for gambling
- Illegal gambling
- Absenteeism from work
- Revenue for state in form of gambling taxes

SUPPORT SERVICES/GROUPS
Gamblers Anonymous, Gam-anon

HOUSING

MAIN PROBLEMS ASSOCIATED WITH HOUSING
- Shortage of suitable, affordable housing
- Segregation of communities, based on house prices
- Large mortgages taken out to provide homes
- Substandard housing resulting from housing shortage
- High rents charged for substandard housing
- Isolation and loneliness in housing estates/apartment blocks
- Lack facilities and amenities in housing estates

EFFECTS ON INDIVIDUALS, FAMILY AND SOCIETY

ON INDIVIDUALS
- Emotional stress and tension
- Economic difficulties
- Inability to pay mortgage or rent
- Poor health due to substandard conditions
- Pressure to work two jobs to pay rents

ON THE FAMILY/CHILDREN
- Anxiety and stress leading to depression
- Breakdown in family relationships
- Overcrowding, no privacy
- Substandard housing cause health problems
- Children leaving home too early
- Problems at school, at work

ON COMMUNITY/SOCIETY
- Homelessness, children or adults on the streets
- Increased pressure on social welfare services
- Increase in crime and delinquency
- Communities begin to form residence groups

HOMELESSNESS

People without homes living on the streets are defined as homeless.

FACTORS CONTRIBUTING TO HOMELESSNESS

- Breakdown of relationships with family members
- Marital breakdown
- Unemployment
- Poor educational achievement, but not in all cases
- Physical or mental illness
- Shortage of affordable housing
- Release from prison or psychiatric hospitals

EFFECTS ON INDIVIDUALS, FAMILY AND SOCIETY

ON INDIVIDUALS

- Loss of identity
- Separation from family and friends
- Experience of prejudice
- Poor health due to the living conditions
- Little privacy, no storage for belongings
- Loss of dignity and self-esteem

ON THE FAMILY

- Loss of contact with family member
- Constant worry, fear and tension
- Shame and guilt

ON SOCIETY

- Increase in vagrancy, people begging
- Increase in crime
- Demands on voluntary agencies

SUPPORT SERVICES/GROUPS

Focus Point, Residents Associations, Simon Community, Salvation Army, St. Vincent de Paul.

POVERTY

Poverty is defined within a cultural context and the strength of a country's economy.

FACTORS CONTRIBUTING TO POVERTY
- Unemployment
- Poor quality housing conditions
- The poverty trap
- Large families
- Leaving school early, low level of skills
- Low paid jobs
- Inadequate retirement pensions
- Poor agricultural lands
- Migrant communities, irregular employment

SUPPORT SERVICES/GROUPS

Agencies combatting poverty, Combat Poverty Agency, St. Vincent de Paul, Focus Point, Enterprise Schemes for Small Businesses, Social Employment Schemes, area-based Partnership Projects, Family Income Supplement, Second Chance Education, grants, subsidies and other EU schemes for farmers.

SUBSTANCE ABUSE

ALCOHOL AND ALCOHOL ABUSE

ALCOHOL
- is a depressant drug which the body absorbs very quickly into the bloodstream
- is a socially accepted drug which when abused can result in alcoholism
- abuse can leads to physical and psychological dependence

FACTORS CONTRIBUTING TO ALCOHOL ABUSE
- Socially accepted drug
- Easily available
- Peer pressure, need to belong
- Low self-esteem
- Has relaxing effects

EFFECTS OF ALCOHOL ABUSE ON INDIVIDUALS, FAMILY AND SOCIETY

ON THE INDIVIDUAL
- Drink-driving can cause death of others
- Denial, individuals 'do not have a problem'
- Financial problems
- Absenteeism from work and from family
- Unemployment, loss of job
- May lead to fraud and stealing from others
- Deterioration of co-ordination, speech and vision
- No inhibitions, personality changes
- Becomes violent towards others, relationships change

ON THE FAMILY
- Possible violence in the home
- Financial difficulties, no money available for food and bills
- Breakdown in relationships, breakup of family
- Loss of family home, poverty
- Loss of job of main earner/bread winner
- Loss of confidence among children, neglect of children
- Poor role model for family members

ON COMMUNITY/SOCIETY
- Increased deaths on the roads due to drink driving
- Absenteeism from work places
- Violence and rows in public places
- Increased demands on the social welfare system
- Increased poverty in community
- Misuse of social welfare payments

SUPPORT SERVICES/GROUPS

Alcoholics Anonymous, Alateen, Al-anon, Specialised Centres, Hospitals

DRUGS AND DRUG ABUSE

ABUSE OF DRUGS
- Leads to physical, psychological and social dependence
- Results in addiction when the individual is unable to control the craving for the drug
- Causes withdrawal symptoms when the drug is not taken

Classification of Drugs

Hallucinogens	Cannabis, LSD, solvents
Opiates	Heroin
Sedatives	Alcohol, tranquillizers
Stimulants	Amphetamines, caffeine, cocaine, nicotine

FACTORS CONTRIBUTING TO DRUG ABUSE

- Peer pressure among young people
- Availability and use of drugs at home
- Boredom, stress, pressure, excitement
- Body needs the drug or withdrawal symptoms will occur
- Doing badly at school, leaving early and taking drugs
- For adults, stress at work
- Homelessness

EFFECTS OF DRUG ABUSE ON INDIVIDUAL, FAMILY, SOCIETY

On the Individual

- Health problems (physical and psychological)
- Leaving school early, poor school work
- Relationship problems, breakdown of relationships
- Dependency on the drug, leading to death
- Personality changes, mood swings, emotional turmoil
- Involvement in criminal activities e.g. selling drugs
- Possible criminal record
- Risk of developing and dying from AIDS

On the Family

- Constant fear, tension and rows
- Loss of family member if drug abuser dies
- Abuse of spouse and children or siblings
- Economic problems, unemployment
- Health problems associated with malnutrition
- Bad example for other members of the family
- House searches if drug addict becomes a dealer
- Stigma, social outcasts, may have to move home

On Community/Society
- People living in fear of drug addicts and pushers
- Instability in communities
- Increase in criminal activity
- Community groups coming together to fight the problems
- Increase in unemployment in community
- Spread of AIDS, hepatitis and other diseases
- Increased demands on health and welfare services

SUPPORT SERVICES/GROUPS

Welfare Services, Psychiatric Hospitals, Drugs Advisory and Treatment Centre, Coolmine Treatment Centre, Department of Health

17

CHILD DEVELOPMENT AND EDUCATION

CHILD DEVELOPMENT

The family is the primary centre for early child care and development. Children live within the context of family, community and society.

KEY AREAS OF DEVELOPMENT

Physical development through:
- Healthy safe home environments
- Healthy balanced diets
- Adequate time for exercise, rest and play

Co-ordination or motor development through:
- Learning how to control and co-ordinate movement
- Opportunities for development of fine motor skills
- Playing with toys
- Helping parents and siblings with simple tasks
- Exploring the world around them

Socialisation development through:
- Relationships with parents, siblings, child minders
- Relationships with friends
- Language and vocabulary development
- Learning to share and help

Personality development through:
- Getting to know self, developing a sense of identity
- Expanding experience of their world
- Developing confidence, self-esteem
- Learning skills of responsibility and tolerance
- Learning to control their own behaviour
- Spiritual development

Development of Intelligence through:
- Opportunities to develop individual abilities
- An enriched home environment e.g. books
- Supportive and encouraging family
- An adequate education system

EDUCATION

FACTORS INFLUENCING EDUCATIONAL ACHIEVEMENT
- Good parenting, parental support
- Family attitudes and value
- Family size and situation
- Home and community environment
- Attitudes of peer group
- Parental relationships with school
- Educational achievement of parents

PURPOSES OF EDUCATION

- Development of personality
- Social development in a protected environment
- Socialisation of child among their peers
- Economic, to prepare them for the future

EDUCATIONAL EXPERIENCES OUTSIDE THE HOME

PRE-SCHOOL PLAY GROUPS

- Children not obliged to attend a pre-school play group
- Pre-schools may be private or voluntarily
- Pre-schools must register with the local health board
- Child Care Regulations must be implemented and enforced
- Pre-schools must be healthy, hygienic and safe environments

ASSESSING THE SUITABILITY OF A NURSERY OR CRÉCHE

Organised pre-school activities assist in the social, physical and intellectual development of young children. When selecting a pre-school nursery or créche parents should:

- Ask family and friends about their experiences with the créche
- Visit the pre-school or créche
- Check that it has been registered with the Health Board
- Check that the regulations of the Child Care Act 1991 and Child Care (Pre-school) Regulations 1996 are practised
- On the visit try to decide if children are happy and well cared for by the staff
- Check that it is clean, well-maintained and suitable for the age group
- Visit play and rest areas
- Ask about arrangements for mealtimes
- Arrangements for record keeping on children

EARLY START PRE-SCHOOL PROGRAMME

- Developmental educational programme, laying a solid foundation for the future
- Set up in areas of particular disadvantage
- Primary school teachers, child care assistants, pupils and parents work together

PRIMARY SCHOOL
- State-assisted National Schools, mainly denominational
- Curriculum is child-centred and set
- Some private primary schools, parents pay fees
- Activity-based teaching and learning methods are used
- Lays a foundation for the child's development
- Considers individual differences, interests and needs

POST PRIMARY SCHOOL
- Community schools, comprehensive schools, secondary schools, vocational schools
- Ownership and management structures differ
- Consists of 5–6 years

SUMMARY OF PROGRAMMES ON OFFER

Junior Certificate Programme, Transition Year Programme, Leaving Certificate Programmes (Leaving Certificate, Leaving Certificate Applied, Leaving Certificate Vocational Programme)

OPPORTUNITIES AFTER LEAVING CERTIFICATE

Opportunities include Post Leaving Certificate Courses, Apprenticeships, Third-Level Education, Adult Education and Vocational Training Scheme, Back to Education Programmes.

EDUCATIONAL ADVISORY BODIES

Educational Advisory Bodies include Teastas, Higher Education Authority, National Council for Education Awards (NCEA), National Council for Curriculum and Assessment (NCCA) and the National Centre for Guidance in Education.

RECENT DEVELOPMENTS IN EDUCATION

- Back to Education Programmes
- More time spent in school
- Increased involvement of parents, employers and community
- Opportunities for work experience at second level
- Revision of programmes at Junior and Senior Cycle
- Scientific and Technological Education (Investment) Fund
- Schools IT 2000 Initiative
- National Psychological Service
- Home School Community Liaison Scheme
- Introduction of TY in most schools

18

COMMUNITY AND COMMUNITY ISSUES

OUR COMMUNITY

Communities consist of families and individuals living on the same road, in the same town, in the same rural townland or on the same island. They are neighbours, some belonging to the area for many generations, others new to a community and just getting to know their neighbours. There are differences between traditional communities and modern communities. Some communities have a mix of social classes, age groups and occupations. Others are less mixed for a variety of reasons e.g. cost of housing. Communities help to form groups that improve the living conditions for people in their area and plan for further development of their area.

EXAMPLES OF COMMUNITY GROUPS

- Citizen Information Centres
- Community-based Health Services (doctors, dentists, etc.)
- Community Councils, Development Groups
- Local Heritage Group
- Neighbourhood Watch and Community Alert
- Macra Na Feirme
- Pressure Groups to deal with specific community issues
- Residents Associations
- Tidy Town Group
- Toddler Groups (voluntary)

SCHEMES TO ASSIST COMMUNITY DEVELOPMENT

- Area Partnership Companies
- Urban and Rural Renewal Development

ADVANTAGES OF LOCAL GROUPS

Setting up local groups:
- Helps improve the living conditions within the area
- Improves the environment
- Develops expertise within the community
- Forms links with state services e.g. Gárdaí
- Develops and strengthens community relationships
- Sets an example for young people
- Provides volunteers to supplement state services
- Increases local knowledge about community needs
- Brings about changes through pressure groups

THE ELDERLY IN OUR COMMUNITY

- People are living longer
- Improved nutrition, health care and living conditions
- Planning for retirement by paying into pension funds
- Caring for the elderly is an important responsibility

PROBLEMS ASSOCIATED WITH OLD AGE

- Inadequate financial planning for retirement
- Physically aging, the body slows down
- Poor diet, loss of interest in food, unable to go shopping
- Health problems e.g. heart disease, cancer, arthritis
- Hypothermia
- Loss of confidence, feeling insecure
- Loneliness, family move away, close friends die
- Loss of respect for the elderly
- Moving in with family, conflict with family
- Unsuitable housing for old age
- Refusing to have home help

SUPPORT AVAILABLE FROM

- Friendly relatives or neighbours
- Active Age Clubs and Groups
- Association of Services for the Aged
- Day Care Centres
- Friends of the Elderly
- Nursing Homes, Residential Care (private and state)
- Regular Meals on Wheels

- Regular visits from the public health nurse
- Sheltered Accommodation
- State Health Service/Community Care

SOCIAL WELFARE BENEFITS FOR THE ELDERLY
- Pensions, allowances for electricity, gas, free telephone rental and TV licence, free travel and food vouchers

PEOPLE WITH DISABILITY IN OUR COMMUNITY

A disability is a limitation of physical or mental ability that interferes with the everyday life of an individual e.g. loss of sight, co-ordination problems, impaired development of the mind.

EDUCATIONAL SERVICES
- Schools for students who are unable to attend the local primary school
- Special arrangements in primary schools for individual pupils e.g. assistants, physical changes to the school building (ramps)
- Special schools at second level for pupils with learning difficulties
- Special arrangements for students with specific physical disability
- Special aids e.g. laptop computers

Other education services include Diagnostic Assessment and Advisory Services, remedial teaching, speech therapy, home tuition, visiting teachers.

TRAINING PROGRAMMES
A variety of local and national training programmes are provided by a range of state and non-governmental organisations e.g. FÁS, CERT and Teagasc. National training programmes are provided.

COMMUNITY-BASED SERVICES
Provided by the Health Board to include home help, therapy (occupational, physiotherapy, speech), public health nursing service and social work service.

SUPPORT SERVICES/GROUPS
National Social Services Board, Department of Education and Science, Central Remedial Clinic, National Medical Rehabilitation Centre, FÁS, Rehab Group, AHEAD, Centre for Independent Living, Disabled Drivers Association, Irish Council of People with Disabilities, Irish Deaf Society, Mental Health Association, National Council for the Blind of Ireland, Health Boards.

Training and Employment
- Community Employment Programme
- Disability Federation of Ireland
- National Rehabilitation Board (training and employment)
- Public Service (% reserved for people with disabilities)
- Sheltered Workshops

Problems Associated with Disability
- Integration into local schools
- Family finance inadequate to cope with the needs
- Integration in the workplace
- Access to buildings, buses and trains
- Attitudes in society to disability

DEPRIVED CHILDREN IN OUR COMMUNITY

Problems Associated with Deprived Children
Emotional, physical and sexual abuse, disability, early school leavers, homelessness, neglect by parents, poverty, poor home environment and malnutrition

Factors Contributing to Child Neglect
Abuse, alcoholism, drug abuse, poor educational achievement, breakup of family, irresponsible parents, financial problems (gambling), poor housing and violence in the home

Assistance Available
Assistance is available from Childline, Day Care Centres for young children, Fostering (children in care, long-term or short-term), Health Boards, Irish Society for the Prevention of Cruelty to Children, Residential homes (children in care), Parents Under Stress, Social Work Services and Child Guidance Services.

YOUTH IN OUR COMMUNITY

Adolescence is accompanied by so many changes that the transition from childhood to adulthood is difficult. A distinct youth culture has developed, so that teenagers identify with specific attitudes, beliefs, dress, language, music, symbols and values.

CHANGES IN ADOLESCENCE

Changes may cause difficulties between adolescent and parents. Parents watch as their child grows from childhood dependency to adulthood independence, sometimes finding it difficult to let go. The main changes are:
- Independence (personal and financial)
- Physical and emotional changes
- Development of new friendships/relationships
- Peer pressure

PROBLEMS ASSOCIATED WITH ADOLESCENCE

- Emotional and physical changes
- Identity crisis, not a child, not yet an adult
- Difficulties in relationships, parents and peers
- Decision making
- External pressures from peer group, gangs
- Drugs and alcohol
- Influence of mass media and advertising

YOUTH WORK

Young people can play a responsible part in their community through youth organisations.

By working as volunteers young people develop their skills, attitudes and values so that they become responsible citizens. Boredom is avoided and they are less likely to become involved in undesirable activities. Leadership qualities are developed.

EXAMPLES OF YOUTH ACTIVITIES

An Gaisce, Summer Projects, Youth Information Centres, Youth Clubs and Youth Work Services

EXAMPLES OF YOUTH ORGANISATIONS

Catholic Youth Council, Community Games, Foróige, Girl Guides, Scouts

19

OUR WORLD TODAY

SOME ISSUES FACING SOCIETY

- Technological developments
- Gender equality
- Changing world of work
- Employment and unemployment
- Demographic trends, urbanisation
- Rural migrations
- Emigration and migration
- Mass media
- Advertising
- Leisure
- Gaps between rich and poor nations

THE CHANGING WORLD OF WORK

Everyone has the right to work. Factors that influence our attitudes to work are family background, community, economic trends, educational achievements, school attended, social group and the skills demanded in the workplace. A job for life is no longer the norm. Contract work is common among the younger age group. Fewer people are getting a permanent, pensionable job for life as in the past. Technology skills are essential for most jobs today.

REASONS FOR WORKING

- Provides clothing, food and shelter (basic needs)
- Makes individuals and families independent
- Satisfies psychological and social needs
- Confers respect and status
- Is a measure of success in life
- Develops self-esteem and confidence
- Provides interest and satisfies basic drives within us

REASONS FOR MARRIED WOMEN WORKING

- Changes in traditional roles, more sharing of roles
- Independence for women
- Equality in the workplace
- Confers status, is a measure of success
- Provides extra money to pay basic bills
- Improves standard of living
- Pays for luxuries (holidays)
- Partners share financial burdens
- Breakup of family and family home
- Desire to develop a career outside the home

CHANGES IN THE WORLD OF WORK

- Technological advances and developments
- Move towards lifelong learning and training
- Opportunities for study leave
- Gender equality in the workplace
- Job sharing
- Maternity/paternity leave arrangements
- Better working conditions, new health and safety regulations
- Increased consultation between management and workers
- Improved wages and pension arrangements

CHANGES IN THE COMMUNITY

- Increased need for child care services
- Dual-career families
- Increase in number of women in the workplace
- Increased emphasis on what is success (job, house, money)
- Increased family mobility
- Breakdown in family structures
- Traffic problems (grid-lock, noise, pollution)
- Travelling greater distances to work
- New buildings and roads
- Influences of new technologies

LEGISLATION AND ORGANISATIONS

Improvement in the conditions in the workplace have been brought about by:
- Charter of Rights for Workers within the Social Chapter of the Maastricht Treaty 1991
- Protection of Young Persons (Employment) Act 1996
- Council for the Status of Women
- Employment Equality Agency
- Unions

UNEMPLOYMENT

FACTORS INFLUENCING UNEMPLOYMENT INCLUDE

- Changes in the economy
- Companies and businesses closing down
- Companies transferring to cheaper labour economies
- Leaving school early, education incomplete
- Seasonal adjustments
- Technological developments, new skills required
- Unskilled workers, need to be up-skilled
- People consider themselves better off on social welfare

EFFECTS OF UNEMPLOYMENT ON INDIVIDUAL, FAMILY AND SOCIETY

On the Individual
- Sense of rejection following each unsuccessful interview
- Financial problems, worry about bills
- Relationship problems, rows, strained relationship
- Lowering of social status
- Decline in self-esteem and confidence

On the Family
- Health problems
- Children may suffer emotionally and psychologically
- Can shape children's view of employment/unemployment
- Financial problems leading to poverty
- Tension, possibly violence in the home
- May interfere with children's education

On Community/Society
- Continuation of the 'Black Economy'
- Emigration, migration
- Increase in criminal activity
- Lowering of living standards in the community
- Unstable communities with high unemployment levels
- Increased demands made on the state and the tax payers

Assistance is available through
- The education system, retraining
- Back to Work Allowance Scheme
- Employment Grant for Self-employed
- FÁS back to work training schemes
- Pre-Employment Programmes
- Local Area/Enterprise Initiatives
- Urban and Rural Development Programmes

MIGRATION AND EMIGRATION

FACTORS INFLUENCING MIGRATION AND EMIGRATION

- New Employment or better prospects
- Attain a better standard of living
- Decentralisation of work (Government Departments)
- Getting away from the poverty trap
- Fewer opportunities in rural areas

PROBLEMS ASSOCIATED WITH MIGRATION AND EMIGRATION

- Rural or community depopulation
- Change in age profile in rural communities
- Loneliness and isolation in the depopulated areas
- Breakup of traditional family structures
- Overcrowding in urban areas, insufficient housing
- More agricultural land being rezoned as residential
- Increase in problems associated with large urban areas
- Cut back on services and facilities in rural areas

STEPS TAKEN BY THE GOVERNMENT TO SUPPORT RURAL AREAS

- Decentralisation of government offices
- FÁS training programmes
- Enterprise grants
- Tourism schemes (agri-tourism)

PROBLEMS ASSOCIATED WITH INCREASED URBANISATION

- Insufficient housing, overcrowding
- Poverty, crime, and drugs
- Stress and tension, loneliness
- Environmental pollution
- Traffic problems e.g. 'Gridlock'

STEPS TAKEN BY GOVERNMENT TO SUPPORT URBAN AREAS

- Improving housing
- Extra land zoned for housing developments
- Action taken against drug pushers
- Local employment initiatives
- Improvements in amenities e.g. open spaces
- Traffic freeflow to ease 'gridlock'
- Grants for local enterprises
- Education, FÁS training programmes

THE MEDIA

Developments in technology have resulted in magazines, newspapers, radio and television bringing us information and news from around the world. Globalization has resulted from technological advances. The developments of interactive technology will change our lives.

ADVANTAGES OF THE MEDIA

- Provides education and information
- Provides entertainment
- Expands one's view of the world
- Highlights social issues
- Brings other cultures and languages into our homes

DISADVANTAGES OF THE MEDIA

- Encourages materialism
- Promotes a false image of reality
- Encourages passivity (may change with interactive TV)
- Influences attitudes, beliefs and values
- Easily abused by those who control it

ADVERTISING

Advertising is regulated by the Advertising Standards Authority for Ireland. Legislation controls standards. All advertisements should be honest, legal and truthful and should not be misleading.

ADVERTISING MEDIA

Includes billboards, bus shelters, cinema, clothing (labels), directories, direct mail, Internet, e-mail, e-commerce, products (pens, posters), radio, television, sponsorship.

ADVANTAGES OF ADVERTISING

- Increases awareness of products and services
- Informs the public about new ideas, products, services
- Provides information on jobs, housing, cars, etc.
- Encourages consumer demand
- Creates competition
- Provides employment in a variety of areas

DISADVANTAGES OF ADVERTISING

- Adds to the cost of all products
- Can be misleading
- Creates expectations, sometimes unrealistic
- Encourages dissatisfaction with lifestyle
- Encourages people to buy products they do not need
- Exploits consumers
- May undermine attitudes, beliefs and values

LIFESTYLE AND LEISURE

A balanced lifestyle includes some leisure activities. Education for leisure begins with parents at home. Education for leisure is provided through school, clubs, scouts and other groups. People have more time available for leisure because of technology.

PURPOSES OF LEISURE

- Maintains a healthy body and mind
- Promotes a sense of well-being
- Provides relaxation and opportunities to unwind
- Relieves stress and tension
- Sets good example for children
- Encourages social, personal and professional development

TYPES OF LEISURE ACTIVITIES

Physical: cycling, health clubs, hill walking, sports, swimming
Sedentary: chess, hobbies, painting, reading
Others: debates, drama, quizzes, visiting museums, galleries

20

PREVIOUS QUESTIONS TO PRACTICE

It is important to practice answering past examination questions. A selection of previous questions are outlined below to enable questions and topics to be worked on together during revision.

Nutrients (Question 1 of year)
- Protein 1994, 1990
- Carbohydrates 1995, 1988
- Lipids 1998, 1991
- Minerals 1996, 1993
- Vitamins 1997, 1992, 1987
- Additives 1989, 1996
- Water 1993

PREVIOUS QUESTIONS TO PRACTICE

Planning Balanced Diets (Question 2 of year)
- Variety of diets 1996, 1989
- Teenagers (healthy eating) 1995
- High fibre 1992
- Vegetarian 1991
- Low-cholesterol 1988

Nutrition of Food
- Meat Q.4 1994, Q.2 1990
- Fish Q.4 1992
- Eggs Q.2 1998, Q.4 1993, Q.2 1987
- Cheese Q.2 1994, Q.4 1988
- Cereals Q.4 1996, Q.4 1990
- Pastry Q.4 1997, Q.2 1993
- Yeast Q.4 1998

Microbiology/Food Contamination/Food Preservation
- Q.2 1997, Q.4 1995, Q.2 1991, Q.4 1989, Q.4 1987

Human Physiology (Question 3 of year)
- Pancreas 1998
- Respiratory system 1997
- Nervous system 1996, 1990
- Urinary system 1995, 1991
- Reproduction (female) 1994, 1988
- Reproduction (male) 1989
- Endocrine system 1993
- The liver 1992, 1987

Housing and Services
- Housing Q.9 1997, Q.8 1992, Q.9 1989
- Housing for the elderly Q.7 1995
- Insulation Q.7 1989
- Water (systems/heating) Q.7 (iii) 1997, Q.7 1996, Q.7 1990
- Sanitation and drainage Q.7 1993
- Central heating Q.8 1993, Q.7 1989
- Electricity Q.7 1991
- Lighting Q.9 1994
- Ventilation Q.8 1998

Interior Design and Room Planning
- Colour schemes/paints Q.9 1998
- Interior/wall coverings Q.9 1995
- Kitchens Q.8 1996, Q.9 1992
- Floors/floorings Q.8 1991
- Interior/living rooms Q.9 1988

Appliances
- Dishwasher Q.7 1998, Q.7 1992
- Cleaning appliances Q.8 1997, Q.7 1994
- Ovens Q.8 1995
- Electric appliances Q.7 1991
- Refrigerators Q.8 1990
- Food preparation Q.8 1989
- Microwave/conventional ovens Q.7 1988

Consumer/Money Management
- Q.7 1997, Q.8 1994, Q.9 1993, Q.9 1991, Q.9 1990

Family
- Q.6 1995, Q.5 1993, Q.5 1990

Marriage
- Q.5 1996, Q.5 1993, Q.6 1990

Problems in Family and Society
- The Elderly Q.6 1997
- Poverty, child deprivation Q.5 1995
- Delinquency and crime Q.6 1994
- Drug abuse Q.6 1993
- Child neglect Q.6 (ii) 1991
- Alcohol abuse Q.5 1989
- Poverty Q.5 1988

Child Development and Education
- Pre-school Q.6 1998, Q.6 1988
- Education Q.5 1997
- Adult Education Q.6 (i) 1991

The Community
- Elderly in community Q.6 1997
- Adolescence Q.6 1992
- Disability Q.5 1991
- Youth organisations Q.6 1990

Work and Leisure
- Work/leisure Q.5 1998
- Work/technology Q.6 1996
- Work Q.5 1994
- Unemployment Q.5 1992

PAST EXAMINATION PAPERS

AN ROINN OIDEACHAIS AGUS EOLAÍOCHTA
LEAVING CERTIFICATE EXAMINATION, 2000

HOME ECONOMICS (SCIENTIFIC AND SOCIAL) — HIGHER LEVEL

THURSDAY, 15 JUNE — MORNING, 9.30 TO 12.15

(400 MARKS)

Five questions to be answered.
Two questions must be chosen from **each** Section, the other question at choice of candidate.
All questions carry equal marks.

SECTION I — SCIENTIFIC

1. Give an account of the chemical structure of carbohydrates.
   Describe the properties of (**i**) sugars; (**ii**) starch and (**iii**) cellulose.
   Explain how the energy value of food is calculated and include reference to the energy value of protein, fat and carbohydrate.
   Explain **each** of the following: metabolism; basal metabolic rate; kilocalorie.

2. Discuss the nutritive and dietetic value of meat.
   Outline the factors that affect the toughness of meat and describe a variety of methods used to tenderise meat.
   Using beef **or** lamb, give instructions for preparing, cooking and serving a main course dish suitable for a celebration dinner for four teenagers.
   Write a brief note on vacuum packed meat.

3. Give a detailed account of (**a**) the position, (**b**) the structure and (**c**) the function of the male reproductive system. Use a labelled diagram to illustrate your answer.

Explain the function of **each** of the following (**i**) oestrogen;
(**ii**) progesterone; (**iii**) testosterone.

4. Explain how bacterial food poisoning occurs.
   Name and describe **two** bacteria which cause food poisoning and state the sources and method of infection in each case.
   Using fresh ingredients, describe in detail how you would prepare a chicken casserole **or** pie suitable for freezing. State how the frozen dish should be defrosted and prepared for serving.

SECTION II — SOCIAL

5. Adolescence is a stage of development which brings many changes and pressures.
   Give an account of some of the changes and pressures that young people may have to deal with during adolescence.
   Discuss the contribution that youth work can make towards the development of young people.
   Summarise the factors that should be considered when setting up a youth club and state the characteristics necessary for effective leadership.

6. Ireland is among the EU countries with a high level of relative poverty.
   Define the terms *absolute poverty* and *relative poverty.*
   Give an account of (**i**) the causes and (**ii**) the effects of poverty as exists in modern Ireland.
   Name and describe **three** Government strategies designed to alleviate poverty.
   Write a brief account of the functions of the Combat Poverty Agency.

7. Summarise the main factors that affect a person's choice of housing.
   Set out the results of a study you have carried out on social/local authority housing.
   Refer to **each** of the following:
   (i)   the factors that determine eligibility;
   (ii) the range of housing provided;
   (iii) how rent is calculated;
   (iv) **two** schemes operated by local authorities that enable persons to purchase their own homes.

8. Assess the value of microwave cookers. Include reference to the different types available including combination cookers.
   State the microwave cooker you would recommend for a family kitchen. Give a full account of the appliance and refer to: **(i)** structure; **(ii)** working principle; **(iii)** care and cleaning; **(iv)** modern features; **(v)** cost.
9. List the features of a good household drainage system.
   Give an illustrated account of a household drainage system and state the function of **(a)** the vent pipe and **(b)** the inspection chamber.
   Outline the role of **(i)** the consumer and **(ii)** local authorities in dealing with the growing waste disposal problem.
   Name and outline the activities of **one** organisation that deals with environmental issues.

AN ROINN OIDEACHAIS AGUS EOLAÍOCHTA

LEAVING CERTIFICATE EXAMINATION, 2000

HOME ECONOMICS (SCIENTIFIC AND SOCIAL) — ORDINARY LEVEL

THURSDAY, 15 JUNE — MORNING, 9.30 TO 12.15

(400 MARKS)

Five questions to be answered.
One question must be chosen from **each** Section, the other questions at choice of candidate.
All questions carry equal marks.

SECTION I — SCIENTIFIC

1. Explain why it is important to include iron rich foods in the diet.
   List the dietary sources of iron.
   Design a set of menus for one day for a teenager who has been advised to increase his/her iron intake.
   Write an informative note on the use of dietary supplements.

2. Give an account of the nutritive and dietetic value of milk.
   Describe the processing method used in the production of (i) pasteurised milk **or** (ii) dried milk.
   State the causes of spoilage in milk and explain how spoilage can be prevented.
   Using milk as a main ingredient, give full directions for preparing a nutritious drink **or** dessert suitable for children.

3. Describe, with the aid of labelled diagrams, the respiratory system. Refer to the position and structure of each part.
   Explain how the exchange of gases takes place in the lungs.
   List the factors that affect the rate of breathing.

4. Compile a set of practical guidelines that should be followed when planning meals for elderly persons.
   List **three** nutrients which are particularly important for older people and state why each is important.
   Give full directions for preparing, cooking and serving a low-fat main course dish suitable for two elderly persons.

SECTION II — SOCIAL

5. Despite the current economic success many remain unemployed.
   Give an account of the reasons for unemployment in Ireland today and state the categories of person most likely to be without work.
   Describe the effects of unemployment on (i) the individual; (ii) the family; and (iii) society.
   Describe **one** Government scheme designed to help tackle unemployment.

6. Write an informative account of any **two** of the following:
   (i) the causes and effects of alcohol abuse;
   (ii) the advantages and the disadvantages of urban living;
   (iii) the factors which influence educational achievement;
   (iv) the advantages and disadvantages of the media.

7. Name the most common types of water pollutants.
   State how local authorities treat water in order to ensure that it is safe to drink.
   Describe **one** system of heating water for general domestic use. Illustrate your answer with a labelled diagram.
   State (i) the cause and (ii) the effects of hardness in water.

8. Outline the general factors that should be considered when designing the layout of a new kitchen.
   Show, by labelled diagram, the layout of the kitchen you would recommend for a family home.
   Describe **(i)** the storage units, **(ii)** the work surfaces and **(iii)** the large appliances you would select. Give reasons for your choice.

9. State **(i)** the advantages and **(ii)** the disadvantages of using credit to purchase household goods.
   Name **three** forms of credit available to the consumer and list the general requirements of a credit agreement.
   Outline the benefits of any **two** of the following: **(a)** private health insurance; **(b)** house insurance; **(c)** Pay Related Social Insurance (P.R.S.I.).

AN ROINN OIDEACHAIS AGUS EOLAÍOCHTA

LEAVING CERTIFICATE EXAMINATION, 2001

HOME ECONOMICS (SCIENTIFIC AND SOCIAL) — HIGHER LEVEL

THURSDAY, 12 JUNE — AFTERNOON, 2.00 TO 4.45

(400 MARKS)

Five questions to be answered.
Two questions must be chosen from **each** Section, the other question at choice of candidate.
All questions carry equal marks.

SECTION I — SCIENTIFIC

1. Give an account of the chemical structure of protein.
   Classify protein according to structure and describe each type of protein mentioned. In relation to protein give a detailed explanation of **(i)** biological value, **(ii)** deamination and **(iii)** denaturation.
   Explain how the following properties are applied in food preparation:
   (a) coagulation and **(b)** elasticity.

2. Assess the value of fruit as a food commodity.
   Set out the results of a study you have undertaken on fruit and refer to:
   (i) classification and examples of each class;
   (ii) the changes that take place in fruit as it ripens;
   (iii) the physical and chemical effects of cooking and processing on fruit.
   Give full directions for the method of preparing and serving a fruit gateau **or** a selection of fruit hors d'oeuvres.

3. Give a detailed account of (i) the position and (ii) the structure of the human liver.
   Use labelled diagrams to illustrate your answer.
   Describe blood circulation in the liver.
   Explain the role of the liver in relation to (a) metabolism of nutrients and (b) homeostasis.

4. Explain the underlying principles involved in (i) home freezing and (ii) freeze-drying.
   Describe **two** methods of commercial freezing which are commonly used.
   Give full directions for preparing, cooking, packaging and freezing a small quantity of fresh vegetable soup.
   Explain the possible ill-effects that may result if correct procedures are not followed when (a) packaging food for the freezer and (b) defrosting food.

SECTION II — SOCIAL

5. Give an account of (i) the social and (ii) the personal factors that contribute to marriage stability.
   Discuss the effects of marriage breakdown on spouses and children.
   Write an informative account of **two** of the following:
   (i) The Family Law (Divorce) Act 1996;
   (ii) The Judicial Separation Act 1989 amended by the Family Law Act 1995;
   (iii) The Family Mediation Service.

6. The education system has undergone many changes in recent times.
   Give an account of **each** of the following:
   (i) some of the principal features of contemporary education;
   (ii) the variety of educational options now available to students in post-primary schools in Ireland;
   (iii) the factors that affect educational achievement.
   Discuss the reasons for the increase in the number of adults returning to education and give a brief account of **one** agency that supports adults in returning to education.

7. Discuss some modern trends in the development of small kitchen appliances and equipment. Name **two** small kitchen appliances, one that includes a motor and one that includes a heating element, that you would recommend for a family kitchen.
Give a detailed account of **each** appliance and refer to **(i)** construction; **(ii)** modern features; **(iii)** working principle and **(iv)** cost.
In relation to **one** of the appliances, discuss its merits with regard to **(a)** usefulness and **(b)** energy efficiency.

8. Enumerate the functional requirements of flooring for a family living room. Suggest **two** different types of flooring which would be suitable for a living room.
Give a detailed account of **each** under the following headings:
(i) composition; **(ii)** properties; **(iii)** care and cleaning; **(iv)** cost.
State **(a)** the composition and **(b)** the principles underlying the cleansing action of **one** type of floor cleaning agent.

9. Describe, with the aid of a labelled diagram, a household electrical system. Include reference to the function of **(i)** the meter, **(ii)** the mains switch, **(iii)** the fuse box/miniature circuit breakers, **(iv)** the ring circuit.
Explain **each** of the following: **(a)** kilowatt-hour, **(b)** *nightsaver* electricity and **(c)** earth wire.
Describe **one** electrical safety mark.

AN ROINN OIDEACHAIS AGUS EOLAÍOCHTA

LEAVING CERTIFICATE EXAMINATION, 2001

HOME ECONOMICS (SCIENTIFIC AND SOCIAL) — ORDINARY LEVEL

THURSDAY, 12 JUNE — AFTERNOON, 2.00 TO 4.45

(400 MARKS)

<u>Five</u> questions to be answered.
<u>One</u> question must be chosen from **each** Section, the other questions at choice of candidate.
All questions carry equal marks.

SECTION I — SCIENTIFIC

1. Give an account of Vitamin C under **each** of the following headings:
   (i) functions in the diet; **(ii)** main dietary sources; **(iii)** effects of deficiency; **(iv)** properties.
   State how loss of Vitamin C can be minimised when **(a)** storing, **(b)** preparing and **(c)** cooking food.

2. Set out the results of a study you have carried out on meat under the following headings:
   (i) nutritive value;
   (ii) structure;
   (iii) effects of cooking.
   Using a cheaper cut of meat, give directions for preparing, cooking and serving a main course luncheon dish suitable for a family of four.
   Write an informative note on textured vegetable protein (TVP).

3. Give an account of **(i)** the position and **(ii)** the structure of the human heart.
   Use well-labelled diagrams to illustrate your answer.
   Give an account of the circulation of the blood between the heart and the lungs. State the factors that affect heartbeat.

4. Assess **(i)** the nutritional, **(ii)** the dietetic and **(iii)** the economic value of cereals in the diet.
   Describe how pasta is made and name **three** different types of pasta.
   Describe how you would prepare, cook and serve a pasta dish suitable for an evening meal for two students. Cost the dish.

SECTION II — SOCIAL

5. *Under-age drinking is an increasing social problem.* Comment on this statement and list some guidelines for the sensible use of alcohol.
   Give an account of each of the following:
   (a) the short-term and long-term effects of alcohol abuse on the human body and
   (b) the effects of excessive drinking on **(i)** the family and **(ii)** society.
   Describe **one** source of help available to a person who is alcohol dependent.

6. Write an informative account of any **two** of the following:
   (i) the causes and the effects of young people dropping out of school;
   (ii) the advantages of **(a)** youth clubs and **(b)** play groups in the community;
   (iii) the reasons for and the effects of the increasing participation of foreign nationals in the workforce;
   (iv) the social welfare services available to people who are retired/elderly.

7. Compile a set of general guidelines to be followed when drawing up a budget.
   List **(i)** the compulsory deductions and **(ii)** the optional deductions that may be made from an employee's pay.
   Plan and set out a household budget for a family of three persons with a net income of IR£160.00 per week.
   Write an informative account of **(a)** the Medical Card Scheme **or (b)** Family Income Supplement.

8. Summarise the factors that should be considered when planning colour schemes for the home.
   Give the composition of paint and explain the difference between water-based paints and oil-based paints.
   State the advantages of using paint as a wall finish and describe some decorative paint finishes that are currently popular.

9. State why it is important for the consumer to use energy as efficiently as possible.
   Explain the principle of insulation.
   Describe **one** type of insulation suitable for **each** of the following areas in a new house:
   (i) the attic; **(ii)** the walls; **(iii)** the windows and doors.
   Suggest some guidelines that could be followed in order to save energy when
   (a) heating the home and **(b)** using lighting.